My Defender Sets Me Free

My Defender Sets Me Free

Carter and Lauren Trogdon

XULON PRESS

Xulon Press
2301 Lucien Way #415
Maitland, FL 32751
407.339.4217
www.xulonpress.com

Printed in the United States of America.

ISBN-13: 978-1-54565-643-3

My Defender Sets Me Free
Interactive Teaching Devotional

DEFENDER

So if the Son sets you free, you will be free indeed.
(JOHN 8:36)

For:

_____

From:

Lauren & Carter

Date:

2-7-19

Contents

Introduction

Hello, my name is Carter Trogdon, and I am nine years old. Ever since I was little, I have sought after God's heart. When I was three and a half years old, I confessed Jesus as the Lord and Savior of my life and put my faith and trust in Him. When I was around four years old, I started having dreams with Jesus in them. I have always loved to pray, preach, and teach others about Jesus and His great love for us.

For fun, I enjoy reading the Bible, writing stories, coding, computers, telling jokes, reading, and taking guitar lessons. My favorite foods are salmon and salad. In school, my favorite subject is science. Purple is my favorite color, and my favorite song is "Lord, I Need You" by Matt Maher.

Over summer break, my mom and I had the idea to write an interactive teaching devotional for children. To begin, we would sit on our front porch and think of different topics to write about based on what the Lord has taught us over the years. When my mom asked me what we should name the book, I told her that I wanted God to help us name it. After a few days of praying, I knew the title should be called *My Defender Sets Me Free*. You see, Jesus is our defender, and He sets us free by breaking chains that try to hold us back from being who He has created us to be. We pray this book will help others grow strong in the Lord and bring greater understanding to how we can live in the freedom that Christ paid to give us through the power of the Holy Spirit.

There are thirty interactive teaching devotions included, and you can read them daily, weekly, or as often as you would like. As you read each one, ask the Holy Spirit to help you grow in wisdom and understanding. At the end of each entry, there are fun exercises for you to complete (make sure you have a pencil/pen ready). Also, within each devotional, you will notice references to scripture. There are even additional scripture references at the end of each lesson. The scriptures you see listed go along with what you have just read. Feel free to look up each verse if you want to dig deeper into God's Word. We are excited for you to begin reading and hope you enjoy the book as much as we do!

God Makes All Things New

"In the beginning God created the heavens and the earth."
(GENESIS 1:1, NEW INTERNATIONAL VERSION)

The Lord has always loved to create and make new things. He has such a HUGE imagination and is the best inventor and creator that has ever existed! He created the Heavens, the Earth, and everything in them.

When God created the first human beings, Adam and Eve, He created them in His image (see Genesis 1:27). In the Garden of Eden, God met with Adam and Eve and provided everything they needed. God wanted what was best for Adam and Eve, but He also allowed them to make their own choices. If we couldn't make our own choices, we would be like robots. God didn't make us robots; He made us people!

In the Garden of Eden, God told Adam and Eve they could eat from any tree except from the tree of the knowledge of good and evil (see Genesis 2:16–17). However, the serpent tempted Eve to eat from the tree of the knowledge of good and evil. Eve listened to the serpent's voice instead of God's voice and ate the fruit. Adam ate of the fruit as well (see Genesis 3:6).

When Adam and Eve disobeyed God, sin entered into mankind. Immediately after eating the fruit from the tree of the knowledge of good and evil, feelings of fear and shame overwhelmed them, and they hid from God. Adam and Eve could no longer live in the Garden of Eden because of their disobedience. Since that day, every human being has been born into sin (see Genesis 3).

Nevertheless, there is exciting news! Father God sent His son, Jesus, to die in our place. Jesus never sinned, but gave His life on the cross for us so that when we confess with our mouths that Jesus is Lord, and believe in our hearts that God raised Him from the dead, we will be saved (see Romans 10:9). When we accept Jesus as the Lord and Savior of our lives, He puts His Spirit inside of us (see Galatians 2:20). We also become members of God's Kingdom, where we can live free from the curse of sin and forever with Him. As new creations in Christ, God walks and talks with us just like He did in the Garden of Eden before sin entered the world (see 2 Corinthians 5:17).

Exercise

Take a moment to imagine that you are really dirty and need to take a bath to get clean. Rinsing in the bath water makes you clean, and being clean makes you feel refreshed. Picture the dirt washing away down the drain.

Now, think about what water and dirt symbolize spiritually. The dirt symbolizes the times in our lives we have sinned. The Bible says that we have all sinned (see Romans 3:23). Rinsing the dirt off with water symbolizes repenting of our sins, Jesus cleaning us up, and washing our sins away. Jesus died for us, and even though we aren't perfect, the blood of Jesus is more than enough to make us brand new creations. Jesus wants to clean up our hearts, and help us look more and more like Him each day.

"But if we confess our sins to God, he can always be trusted to forgive us and take our sins away."

(1 JOHN 1:9, CONTEMPORARY ENGLISH VERSION)

Salvation Prayer

If you have never asked Jesus to be your Lord and Savior and want to experience new life in Him, pray the prayer below.

Father God,

I admit that I am a sinner. I believe that You sent Your one and only Son, Jesus, to die on the cross for my sins. I confess with my mouth that Jesus is Lord. I believe in my heart that You raised Him from the dead. I ask You to forgive me for my sins. Thank You that I am saved. I welcome Your presence into my life and ask You to lead me, teach me, and help me walk in Your ways. I thank You for the gift of salvation. Jesus is Lord. Amen.

Sincerely, _____ (write your name and date)

If you just prayed that prayer for the first time, welcome into the Kingdom of God! He loves you more than you will ever know. All of Heaven is rejoicing with you! This is such an exciting time, and it is important to tell others about your decision so they can celebrate with you as well.

Write and Pray

Is there anyone you know that doesn't know Jesus? If so, write down their name and pray for them. Talk to God about this person and how you want them to know Jesus as their Lord and Savior. Ask God to reveal His love to them in a new way.

_____

_____

_____

_____

_____

_____

_____

If no one comes to mind, pray for those in the world who have not yet accepted Jesus as their Lord and Savior. You can even ask God to bring someone along their way that can talk with them about Jesus and reveal His great love.

Additional Scripture Study

Genesis 2	Psalm 51:5	Galatians 2:20
Genesis 3	Romans 6:3–4	

My Defender Sets Me Free

"So if the Son sets you free, you will be free indeed."
(JOHN 8:36)

When we place our faith and trust in Christ, we become free through the power of His Spirit. What does this freedom look like? Typically, people think of freedom as being able to do anything they want, but Christian freedom has an entirely different meaning. Of course, God gives us free will to make choices, but when we love the Lord, Jesus sets us free from chains of sin, and His grace gives us the power to live for Him instead of our own selfish ways. King David wrote that true freedom is trying to do what God would want us to do. He said, "I will live in perfect freedom, because I try to obey your teachings" (Psalm 119:45, Good News Translation).

Think about It

Take a moment to imagine a prisoner in jail. Heavy chains are around the prisoner's hands and feet, making it hard for him to move around. He is dressed in a jail uniform and is trapped behind the prison's bars.

Finally, after many long and hard days and nights in jail, the time comes when the judge tells the prisoner that he can go free. The prisoner's chains are removed. He changes clothes and leaves the prison. Once out of jail, he realizes how wonderful it is to live in freedom. He can dress as he wants, eat what he wants, and do what he wants (within the law).

The imagery of the prisoner is similar to living a life without trusting or obeying God. At times, the devil tries to use different tricks against us so that we also feel trapped behind prison bars. Sometimes, we may be tempted to do mean or bad things. Other times, we may allow fear, anger, worry, doubt, shame, guilt, hatred, bitterness, unforgiveness, hopelessness, and so on to overwhelm us. When we continue doing things we know are wrong, believe the enemy's lies, or try to live without God's help, it's like we are chained up in prison. Behind prison bars, the freedom the Lord wants us to enjoy is more difficult to experience because of the chains that try to weigh us down and hold us back.

However, there is good news for us! God is our judge, and Jesus is the defender that holds the keys to set us free! It's the love of Jesus that comes to our defense. When we ask God to forgive and help us, He takes the keys and unlocks our chains! As we walk out of the prison doors, we still must choose between right and wrong. Let's ask the Lord to help us stay free so that we can truly enjoy His goodness and blessings.

"You are free, but still you are God's servants, and you must not use your freedom as an excuse for doing wrong."
(1 PETER 2:16, CONTEMPORARY ENGLISH VERSION)

Story Time

One evening, two baby deer and their mother were in our fenced in backyard. They had come in through an open gate. We quietly snuck outside to get a closer look at the deer family. Suddenly, the deer saw us and got scared. The mother deer quickly ran and jumped over the fence, but the babies could not jump that high. Instead, acting out of panic, they tried to jump through the fence's rod iron bars and got stuck! The babies could not move and were extremely scared. They cried loudly as their mom watched from a distance, wondering what would happen. My parents and a neighbor had to pry the bars open to free the deer. Once released, the babies ran away quickly to the comfort of their mother.

Looking back at what happened, it is obvious that when the deer family saw us, fear took over and caused the babies to get stuck in the fence. They wanted freedom but were trapped and helpless. It was only when someone much stronger came along that the babies were rescued.

This story reminds me of what happens when we become trapped by fear and try to do things in our own strength. At some point in time, we all have been like these baby deer. When we allow the enemy or thoughts not of God to take control, we too can get stuck. This is when we must cry out for help to the Lord so that He can show us how loving and powerful He is. God wants to come to our rescue and give us freedom so that we can run into His arms and find comfort in Him.

"Now the Lord is the Spirit, and where the Spirit of the Lord is, there is freedom."
(2 CORINTHIANS 3:17)

Draw It!

Draw a picture of Jesus as our defender who sets us free.

Additional Scripture References

Isaiah 33:22	John 8:32	Galatians 5:1
Isaiah 61:1	Romans 8:2	Galatians 5:13
Psalm 118:5	Romans 8:16	

Jesus is Our Friend

"There are "friends" who destroy each other,
but a real friend sticks closer than a brother."
(PROVERBS 18:24, NEW LIVING TRANSLATION)

A s Christians, Jesus also calls us His friends, and as His friends, we are called to love God and show God's love to one another (see John 15:17). Jesus wants to be friends with us forever. In fact, He died on the cross so we could be friends with Him now and throughout eternity (see John 15:13).

Jesus loves you so much. Even when times are hard, He is there for you. When you are lonely, afraid, sad, or upset, remember Jesus is with you. He is by your side in the good times and the bad. Jesus thinks you are wonderful, special, and unique. He loves being around you.

Did you know that Jesus is the most loyal and wonderful friend we will ever have? He is dependable, honest, wise, forgiving, loving, respectful, understanding, giving, patient, kind, faithful, humble, thoughtful, trustworthy, and so much more. Who wouldn't want a friend like Jesus? Good friends are a treasure. The Bible tells us that we must choose our friends wisely (see Proverbs 12:26). After all, the more time we spend with our friends, the more we start to act like them. As our friendship with Jesus grows, we start to become the kind of friend He is, and radiate His love to others.

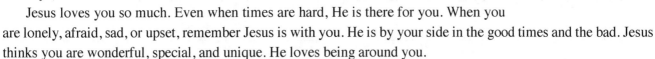

"Do not be misled: "Bad company corrupts good character."
(1 CORINTHIANS 15:33)

Story Time

Have you ever felt left out? Once, I was on a playground with a group of kids. I wanted to play with them, but for some reason, they didn't want to play with me. At first, I felt lonely, but then I remembered that Jesus was with me and I could talk to Him about anything. It was OK that the kids didn't want to play with me.

I had my best friend with me. I love hanging out with Jesus because He understands me and always welcomes me when I come to Him.

"The LORD himself goes before you and will be with you; He will never leave you nor forsake you.
Do not be afraid; do not be discouraged."
(DEUTERONOMY 31:8)

Write about It

Once, I knew Jesus was close by me when

_____

_____

_____

_____

When I know Jesus is with me I feel

_____

_____

_____

_____

Additional Scripture References

Proverbs 17:17   John 15:14–15

Power in the Name of Jesus

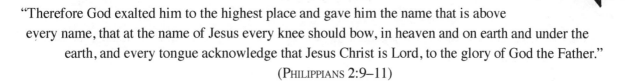

"Therefore God exalted him to the highest place and gave him the name that is above
every name, that at the name of Jesus every knee should bow, in heaven and on earth and under the
earth, and every tongue acknowledge that Jesus Christ is Lord, to the glory of God the Father."
(PHILIPPIANS 2:9–11)

Jesus is the Word of God, and His name is all powerful (see John 1:1,14). Having faith in the Word of God is important. It's not enough to only read the Bible (even people who aren't Christian can do that). Instead, we must read it, and by faith, ask the Lord to help us use the Bible daily to do what it tells us to do. For example, the Bible says to sing to the Lord and bless His name (see Psalm 96:1–2). We shouldn't only read about singing to the Lord and praising His name; instead, we should read it and then do it (see James 2:17). As we practice God's Word, He opens our eyes to show us how beautiful and powerful He is.

One of my favorite stories about the power of Jesus was when He commanded a storm to stop. One day, Jesus and His disciples were on a boat. Jesus was asleep when suddenly, a strong storm formed. The storm was so big that waves began crashing over the boat. The disciples were terrified and woke Jesus up. Jesus stood and told the wind and waves to be still. Immediately, the storm stopped, and everything was calm. The disciples were amazed at Jesus's power. Jesus is so powerful that even the wind and waves obey Him (see Mark 4:35–41).

"No one is like you, LORD; you are great,
and your name is mighty in power."
(JEREMIAH 10:6)

Story Time

Once, I had a dream where I saw the devil, and he was trying to silence my voice. At first, I tried to speak, but only a whisper would come out. In the

21

dream, I prayed and knew to yell out the name of Jesus! After I spoke the name of Jesus, the devil ran away. It was obvious that he understood the power that comes from the name of Jesus.

There is power in the name of Jesus! When we put our faith and trust in Jesus, His power is at work for us and in us (see Ephesians 1:19–20). His breath is in your lungs to boldly declare His Word! You have a strong voice for Jesus so don't let fear, doubt, worry, or anything else silence His voice inside of you.

Write about It

As you do what the Bible tells you to do, you are walking in the power of Jesus. What is something the Bible tells you to do that you have done?

_____

_____

_____

_____

Write about a time you experienced the power of Jesus or read about the power of Jesus in the Bible.

_____

_____

_____

_____

Additional Scripture References

Jeremiah 10:6	Acts 4:12	2 Timothy 1:7
Acts 3:6	Ephesians 3:20	

The Holy Spirit

"But you will receive power when the Holy Spirit comes on you; and you will be my witnesses in Jerusalem, and in all Judea and Samaria, and to the ends of the earth."

(ACTS 1:8)

Jesus is no longer physically on the Earth but is seated at the right side of His Father in Heaven (see Mark 16:19). It must have been hard for Jesus's disciples, friends, and family to say goodbye to Him as He went into Heaven. Jesus told His disciples, "But I tell you I am going to do what is best for you. This is why I am going away. The Holy Spirit cannot come to help you until I leave. But after I am gone, I will send the Spirit to you" (John 16:7, Contemporary English Version).

Wow, can you believe Jesus said it was better for Him to go to Heaven so that we could receive the Holy Spirit? The Holy Spirit is important and helps us in many ways. He comforts, teaches, guides, leads, gives spiritual gifts, holds wisdom, increases our faith, heals, works miracles, prays, protects, encourages, convicts, and does so much more. Also, the Holy Spirit will always point us to Jesus and agree with the Bible; after all, the Holy Spirit worked through many different people to write the Bible (2 Timothy 3:16-17 and 2 Peter 1:21).

Another job of the Holy Spirit is to provide us with the fruit of the Spirit. The fruit of the Spirit isn't real fruit we put in our mouths, but heavenly fruit we feed our spirits. This fruit nourishes us and helps us act more like Jesus. The more we eat of the Holy Spirit's fruit, the stronger we grow spiritually and freer we feel.

"But the Holy Spirit produces this kind of fruit in our lives: love, joy, peace, patience, kindness, goodness, faithfulness, gentleness, and self-control. There is no law against these things!"

(GALATIANS 5:22–23, NEW LIVING TRANSLATION)

Think about It

Finally, the Holy Spirit releases God's Kingdom power (see 1 Corinthians 4:20). Take a moment and think about how electricity works. Have you ever plugged something into an electrical outlet? At times, you can see a spark come out from the outlet, but most of the time, the only way to know electricity is flowing through the outlet is by plugging something in and seeing it work. For example, when a lamp is plugged into a working electrical outlet, power flows through it. The electric flow is what gives power to the lamp so that it can shine brightly and work the way it was designed to.

In a similar way, the Holy Spirit is like the electric power that flows through us from God. If we want to impact the world for Jesus, we must connect with the power of the Holy Spirit. As we do, His power and authority run through us so we can shine brightly for all to see. Connecting to the Holy Spirit's power brings light to the world so others can see that our God is alive and all-powerful (see Matthew 3:11).

"For the kingdom of God is not a matter of talk but of power."
(1 CORINTHIANS 4:20)

Get to Know the Holy Spirit

Would you invite a friend over to your house every day and completely ignore them the entire time? Of course not, because ignoring your friend would make it extremely difficult to get to know them. The same is true with the Holy Spirit. He wants us to get to know Him by talking with Him and applying the Bible to our lives. After all, the more we know the Holy Spirit, the more we grow in Godly wisdom.

Fill in the Blanks

*Love, Joy, Peace, Patience, Kindness,
Goodness, Faithfulness, Gentleness, Self-Control*

A fruit of the Spirit I eat a lot of is

_____

_____

A fruit of the Spirit I would like to eat more of is

_____

_____

I would like the Holy Spirit to teach me more about

_____

_____

Additional Scripture References

Ezekiel 36:26–27	Acts 2:1–21	Romans 12:6–8	Ephesians 1:13
John 14:12	Acts 2:38	1 Corinthians 2:13	
John 14:26	Romans 8:26	1 Corinthians 12:4–11, 28	

God Listens and Speaks

"Call to me and I will answer you and tell you great and unsearchable things you do not know."
(JEREMIAH 33:3)

G od wants to speak to us even more than we want to speak to Him. God speaks in many ways, but the main way He speaks is through the Bible. Prayer is another important way we hear from the Lord. In fact, Jesus spent a lot of time praying to His Father in Heaven and teaching His disciples to pray (see Luke 5:16 and Luke 11:1–4). Prayer is like an invisible phone line that calls God. As we pray, we connect with God, and He hears from us, and we hear from Him.

It is important to understand that prayer is more than memorizing words to repeat over and over again. In fact, what makes prayer special is that it comes from deep within your heart. Many people pray to God, but they don't really mean what they say. Other times, the only reason people pray is so God will do something for them. Of course, God wants to help us, and we should ask for His help in our lives, but we should also ask Him what is on His heart, and thank Him for who He is.

Also, when you pray, remember that God may not answer in the exact way you want Him to. However, trust Him and know that He will answer in the best way He sees for your life (even if it doesn't make sense right away). For example, someone may pray and ask the Lord to help them act more like Jesus. God may respond and have that person work on their patience. Shortly after praying, the person could find themselves in long lines, waiting for things, or surrounded by people who test their patience. At first, it may seem frustrating, but in reality, it is an answer to prayer because God is giving them an opportunity to work on their patience and become more Christ-like (see James 1:2–4).

God really loves it when you spend time with Him, and you should enjoy spending time with God too. He might respond to you in His Word, a vision, dream, nature, a gentle whisper, through people, and so on. Prayer is like calling or writing a letter to your best friend, and God is like a pen-pal that writes back through the Holy Spirit. Your friend, your messenger, God, is the ruler of the entire Universe, and He wants to talk to you.

Story Time

Years ago, my sister and I were playing at a play place. We were having fun climbing and running around, but my sister kept falling down and getting hurt. I didn't like seeing my sister get hurt. Each time she fell down, I would go over to her and pray for the pain to leave. No matter how many times she fell down, I kept praying and asking God to make her feel better.

Later that night, I was relaxing at home when all of the sudden I heard the Holy Spirit say, "Luke 11:9." Even though I didn't know what the verse said, I knew God wanted to speak to me through His Word. When I opened the Bible to Luke 11:9, I noticed the scripture was highlighted! It read, "And so I tell you, keep on asking, and you will receive what you ask for. Keep on seeking, and you will find. Keep on knocking, and the door will be opened to you" (Luke 11:9, New Living Translation). At that moment, I knew the Lord was speaking to me about my prayers. He wanted me to know that when I come to Him in prayer, it is OK to keep asking Him to help no matter how many times I need to ask. He was also telling me to keep seeking Him, and to keep knocking on His door because He is there and wants to answer me.

Write about it

What are some ways you have experienced God speaking to you?

_____

_____

_____

_____

Faith in Action

Ask God to speak to you this week. Write about what you felt the Holy Spirit revealing to you.

_____

_____

_____

_____

_____

_____

_____

_____

_____

_____

Additional Scripture References

2 Chronicles 7:14	Matthew 6:5–8
Psalm 17:6	1 John 5:14
Jeremiah 29:12	

Thankful Hearts of Hope, Joy, and Peace

"May the God of hope fill you with all joy and peace as you trust in him, so
that you may overflow with hope by the power of the Holy Spirit."
(ROMANS 15:13)

As we trust in the Lord, feelings of thanksgiving, joy, peace, and hope fill our hearts. God takes great delight in you. When Jesus died on the cross, He thought of you, and you brought Him great joy (see Hebrews 12:1–2). As we seek God's presence, He fills us with peace and joy. I had an old friend who once told me, "The world will never know peace until it knows the Prince of Peace." When we know Jesus, we can be sure that when we go to Him for help, He will give us peace.

Of course, life is not always easy, and sometimes we go through hard times. However, even in the hard times, we know Jesus is always with us, and in Him, we will find joy, peace, and hope. This is why it is important to worship the Lord in good times and bad. Scripture says that as we come to the Lord, we should enter His gates with thanksgiving and His courts with praise (see Psalm 100:4).

We can always be thankful because thankful hearts are not based on what the news, others, or even our situations say, but on what God says. God says that His plans for us are filled with hope and a future (see Jeremiah 29:11). Offering thanksgiving to God for who He is, all He has done, and all He will do, reveals our great love for Him and welcomes His favor and blessings in our lives.

"Make thankfulness your sacrifice to God, and keep the vows you made to the Most High."
(PSALM 50:14, NEW LIVING TRANSLATION)

Story Time

Have you ever done something kind for someone or had someone do something kind for you? Afterward, you may feel happiness, joy, and warmth inside. Have you ever worshipped the Lord and felt His love and goodness overwhelm you? This is how loving God and loving others can make us feel.

Once I was worshiping God in my car to a song about living in the presence of Jesus. All of a sudden, as I was worshiping, I felt warmth and heat going through my body. I asked my mom why I was feeling this way and she said, "It's the Holy Spirit showing you His love and the warmth of His presence." Experiencing God's presence gave me such love, joy, hope, and peace. God is amazing!

"Therefore, since we are receiving a kingdom that cannot be shaken, let us be thankful, and so worship God acceptably with reverence and awe, for our "God is a consuming fire."
(HEBREWS 12:28-29)

Write about It

Write down three things you are thankful for when you think about God.

_____

_____

_____

Write down three things you are thankful for when you think about your life.

_____

_____

_____

_____

_____

_____

_____

_____

Remember, always try your best to look for the good in every situation. Focus on God's goodness and thank Him for all He has done. Hearts full of thanksgiving and trust in the Lord bring forth showers of love, joy, peace, and hope from above.

"Shout for joy to the Lord, all the earth. Worship the Lord with gladness; come before him with joyful songs."
(PSALM 100:1–2)

Additional Scripture References

Psalm 9:1	Romans 14:17	James 4:8
Psalm 95:2–3	Philippians 4:6–7	
Luke 24:32	Hebrews 6:19	

Submitting to God

"Submit yourselves, then, to God. Resist the devil, and he will flee from you."
(JAMES 4:7)

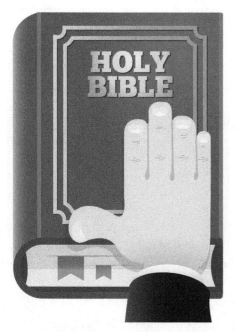

To submit to God means to honor and obey who He is and His ways. The devil doesn't like it when we submit to God because he hates everything about God. In fact, the devil is full of pride and wants to be better than God. He also wants us to think we are better and more important than others. However, God doesn't want us to act like this. Instead, the Bible tells us to treat others as more important than ourselves (see Philippians 2:3).

In scripture, God warns us to be alert because the devil walks around like a roaring lion (see 1 Peter 5:8). You see, the devil is always trying to figure out how to cover up the light of Christ within us. After all, he doesn't want us to be like the One he will never be able to defeat (Jesus).

One of the reasons the devil tries to act like a lion is because he wants to be loud, proud, and in charge. Nevertheless, Jesus is the true lion, and one of His names is the Lion of the Tribe of Judah (see Revelation 5:5). Jesus, the Lion of Judah, is the most powerful, everlasting, eternal King. He is filled with majesty, strength, splendor, and royalty. When we submit to the Lion of Judah, He protects and defends us. His roar is all-powerful, His authority is supreme, and the enemy cannot stand against Him.

"You, dear children, are from God and have overcome them,
because the one who is in you is greater than the one who is in the world."
(1 JOHN 4:4)

Story Time

Once, someone started calling me really mean names. They also told me that I was not smart. At first, their words made me feel sad, but I knew what they were saying about me was not true. Their words reminded me of how the devil roars to try and make us scared or upset. At that moment, I realized that I needed to resist the devil. I didn't want to let the mean words hurt my feelings or cause me to respond unkindly. Instead, I tried to respond in the truth and love of Jesus. Rather than holding onto hurt or saying mean words back, I told the person that I thought they were very smart and that God loved them. The kind words I responded back with seemed to be just what they needed to hear. I even prayed for them.

Looking back, I see how submitting to the Lion of Judah gave me the wisdom to stand up against the roars of untruth. It felt freeing to respond in God's truth and love instead of being hurt by words that were not true. We should not let the mean things others say about us determine who we are. God searches our hearts and hears everything we think and say. Jesus loves to tell us who we are through His eyes, and it is only His opinion of us that truly matters.

It is important to understand how to resist the devil, because not knowing how could cause us to act like him. Sometimes, people are mean because they don't remember or know who Jesus says they are. After all, if they were truly walking in their Christ-given identity, they probably wouldn't want to say or do things that hurt others.

"Do not repay evil with evil or insult with insult. On the contrary, repay evil with blessing,
because to this you were called so that you may inherit a blessing."
(1 PETER 3:9)

Fill in the Blanks

When I mess up or hurt someone's feelings, I feel

_____

_____

_____

When I am reminded that God still loves me, I feel

_____

_____

_____

_____

_____

_____

_____

_____

_____

_____

Additional Scripture References

Job 22:21	Romans 12:8
Luke 6:28	1 Peter 5:6–9
Romans 8:7	

God's Word is Food

"Then Jesus declared, 'I am the bread of life. Whoever comes to me will never go hungry, and whoever believes in me will never be thirsty.'"
(JOHN 6:35)

D id you know that it is important to ask God to make you hungry and thirsty for His Word? You may be asking, "How can we be hungry or thirsty for something that isn't real food or drink?" The Bible says that Jesus is the Word of God and the Bread of Life that gives us living water (see John 1:1 and John 6:35). As we read God's Word and allow the Holy Spirit to help us understand what being a Christian is all about, God begins to feed us by filling us up on the inside.

As Christians, we eat two types of food: real food for our bodies, and spiritual food for our souls. The Bible is our spiritual food! If you had not eaten all day and saw a gigantic plate of delicious food in front of you, would you just sit there and look at it? Of course not, because when you are hungry, and there is food, you want to eat. Not eating can cause your body to be weak or sick.

Now think about your spiritual body. As Christians, we have a hunger deep inside of us to know God more. It's important to feed our spiritual bodies and the main way we do this is by reading the Bible and asking the Holy Spirit to help us apply it to our lives. The Bible also teaches us about the importance of prayer, worship, praise, thanksgiving, love, and so much more. These things also fill us up and bring nourishment to help us grow strong in the Lord.

Finally, reading the Bible isn't about memorizing it so we can look smart in front of others. Doing that would be like taking a piece of bread and rubbing it all over our skin! Bread isn't meant for our skin; it's meant for our stomachs. Many people who aren't Christians can read the Bible and can quote it; the devil even knows the Bible. The difference for us is that as Christians, we read the Bible to know God more because we love Him and want to try our best to do what He tells us to do. As we read the Bible to become who it says we are, we eat the bread of life that fills us up on the inside and gain spiritual strength.

"Jesus answered, "It is written: 'Man shall not live on bread alone, but on every word that comes from the mouth of God.'"

(MATTHEW 4:4)

Story Time

Once, when I was around four years old, I had a dream that I was on a private plane owned by God. I felt like I was sitting in first class and saw Jesus sitting beside me. Jesus was friendly and kind. He wore a beautiful, glowing white robe (see Mark 9:3). Next, I looked in front of me and noticed there was bread on our seat tables. I began to eat bread with Jesus, and drank what seemed like grape juice. I remember Jesus and I spoke to each other. However, we didn't speak through our mouths, but through our hearts. We could understand each other's thoughts. I felt loved and excited to be soaring high with Jesus.

I believe the Lord gave me this dream to show me that He is the Bread of Life. His bright white clothes symbolize His glory and how pure and holy He is. The private plane in the dream represents trusting the Lord and soaring high in the Spirit with Jesus (see Isaiah 40:31). As we spoke, Jesus showed me that even when I pray, He hears me, and I can hear from Him. Finally, eating bread with Jesus and drinking grape juice represents communion. Communion symbolizes having fellowship with Jesus and remembering how He gave His body and His blood so that we could be free from sin and live with Him forever. The bread and juice of Jesus filled me up and gave me delight deep inside my heart. This dream with Jesus is one that I will always remember. I am thankful Jesus reminded me that when we hunger and thirst for Him, He satisfies us with His great love.

Question and Answer Time

What are some of your favorite foods to eat?

_____

_____

_____

_____

What is one of your favorite spiritual foods to eat? (Hint: It could be a book in the Bible, Bible Story, Bible verse, Bible theme, and so on.

_____

_____

_____

_____

_____

_____

Additional Scripture References

Matthew 5:6   John 6:51   John 7:38

God's Love is the Best Gift of All

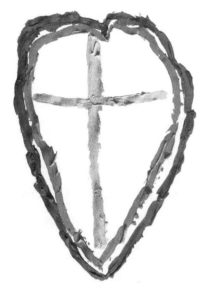

"For God so loved the world that he gave his one and only Son, that whoever
believes in him shall not perish but have eternal life."
(JOHN 3:16)

Jesus never sinned and always stood up for what was right. Even still, many people hated Him and wanted to kill Him. However, Jesus's love was so great that He asked God to forgive those who hurt Him (see Luke 23:34). Jesus gave His life so that everyone could have the opportunity to repent of their sins and make Him their Lord and Savior. Jesus didn't only die on the cross so that we would be with Him one day in Heaven; He also died so that we could get to know Him now through the Holy Spirit living inside of us.

Remembering what Jesus did for us on the cross not only helps us understand how much we have been forgiven; it also helps us understand how much we are worth. God must think we are worth a whole lot if He gave His one and only Son to die for us. We are very special and important to God. When I think about how much God loves me, my heart fills with love for Him.

"Greater love has no one than this: to lay down one's life for one's friends."
(JOHN 15:13)

Think about It

Have you ever felt love in your heart for someone? When you love someone, you think about them often and enjoy spending time with them. The more you love them, the more you want to do the things they like doing because seeing them happy makes you happy. True love wants what is best for the other person, and the same is true with God (see Philippians 2:4).

The more we think about God's love for us and consider our love for Him, the more we think about Him and want to spend time with Him. After all, God created love, and He is love (see 1 John 4:7). The feeling of love we feel for our parents, family, teachers, friends, or pets, is just a small taste of His great love for us. The cross of Jesus is powerful because it symbolizes such amazing love. Whenever you feel like you aren't important, loved, or good enough, remember the cross has spoken and reminds us that we are worth everything to God.

"Anyone who does not love does not know God, because God is love."
(1 John 4:8)

Story Time

A few years back, we saw that a hurricane was about to make landfall a few states down from where we lived. At that time, the people and animals who lived in the path of the hurricane needed to evacuate, and my mom heard that there was a mother dog with young puppies that needed shelter. However, there were so many puppies that the mother and puppies had to split up in groups. Our family wanted to show God's love for those in need by volunteering to take care of three of the puppies.

When the puppies were living with us, I got really attached to them. I felt my love for them grow more and more. One day, the time came to give the puppies to their forever homes. I knew we could not keep them, but I loved them so much. I wanted them to stay with me forever, but I also understood that they were going to homes that would give them even more love and attention. Even still, it was hard to say goodbye to the puppies. My love for them made me miss having them around, but my love for them also helped me say goodbye because I knew they were going to families who would give them wonderful lives.

Faith in Action

Pray to the Lord and ask the Holy Spirit to put someone on your heart that you can show God's love to this week. You could tell them that Jesus loves them, draw them a picture, or give them a hug, compliment, or note to tell them how special they are. Sharing God's love is fun. After all, we love because He loved us first (see 1 John 4:19).

Write the person's name below and the idea the Lord gives you to encourage them with.

_____

_____

_____

_____

_____

_____

_____

_____

_____

_____

_____

Additional Scripture References

Psalm 86:15	1 Corinthians 13:13
John 13:34–35	1 Peter 4:8
Romans 5:8	

Let Your Life Honor the Lord

"You saw me before I was born. Every day of my life was recorded in
your book. Every moment was laid out before a
single day had passed."
(PSALM 139:16, NEW LIVING TRANSLATION)

How amazing is it to know that God saw you even before you were
born? Did you know that God chose you and created you to be
unique and special? You are different than anyone that has ever been
created. No one in the world has the same fingerprints as you, and no one
in the world has the same spiritual fingerprints as you. You could have
been born at any time in the history of the world, but God created you to
be on Earth right now. You could have been born anywhere in the world,
but God knew exactly where you would live.

Your life is a gift from God, and He delights in who you are. The things you are good at (your talents and gifts),
your personality, and what you enjoy are some of the things that make you unique. You were created to touch the
world with the love of Jesus, and you can do it in a way
that no one else can. As you partner with God, He will
help direct you each step of the way.

It pleases God when we honor Him with our actions.
At times, it may be hard to act like Jesus, but we are all
learning and growing. God is very patient with us. The
Bible tells us that King David was known as a man after
God's own heart (see Acts 13:22); however, in Psalms, he
writes about his imperfections for all to see. Even King
David made mistakes, but he would ask God to forgive
him and tried to do better because he loved the Lord.

Like David, even Christians make mistakes, but we should always try our best to set good examples for others. After all, there are people who look up to us and watch what we do. For instance, sometimes kids lie to their moms, dads, teachers, grandparents, friends, or other family members, so they don't get in trouble. Nevertheless, God sees everything. Thank goodness God is merciful and forgiving. If you ask Him for forgiveness and mean it, He will forgive you and forget your sin. Even if you do something wrong, no matter how bad it is, God still loves you and wants you to come to Him for help.

Story Time

Many years ago, a little boy named Billy rode the school bus home with his friend, Tommy. When Billy and Tommy got off the bus, they decided to walk down the street to a small country store to look around. At the store, Tommy saw a pack of bubblegum and decided he was going to steal it, but Billy did not know that Tommy was planning to steal the bubblegum. Later that afternoon when Billy returned home, he found out that the store owner, Mr. Zep, had called his parents and accused him of stealing the bubblegum! You see, Mr. Zep did not know the boys very well and got the two mixed up by mistake.

Even though Billy was innocent, his parents believed Mr. Zep, and Tommy, not wanting to get in trouble, would not admit that he was the one who stole the bubblegum. After the phone call, Billy's dad went down to Mr. Zep's store and paid for the stolen bubblegum. Billy got punished and was told never to go back to the store again.

If Tommy had not stolen from the store or had told the truth after stealing, Billy would not have gotten in trouble or lost the trust of Mr. Zep and his parents. The Bible says, "If you don't do what you know is right, you have sinned" (James 4:17, Contemporary English Version). Telling the truth is always better than telling a lie.

Today, it has been over fifty-five years since Billy got in trouble for stealing the bubblegum, and he still remembers the look of disappointment on his dad's face. You see, the reason I know this is because I know Billy; he is my grandfather.

Think about It

Have you ever done something that you knew was wrong and didn't want your parents or someone else to know about? Why were you afraid to tell the truth?

When we feel like we have to hide what we are doing from others, chances are, we shouldn't be doing those things anyway. After all, Jesus is always in the room watching. Trying our best to do what is right brings honor to Jesus.

Draw Lines to Connect the Words that Go Together from the Left to the Right

Lying   God's Kingdom

Honesty   Not of God's Kingdom

Respect   God's Kingdom

Disrespect   Not of God's Kingdom

Hatred   God's Kingdom

Love   Not of God's Kingdom

Additional Scripture References

Psalm 143:10	1 Corinthians 6:20	Colossians 3:17
Micah 6:8	Ephesians 4:25	Hebrews 10:24

You are God's Masterpiece

"For we are God's masterpiece. He has created us anew in Christ Jesus, so we can do the good things he planned for us long ago."
(EPHESIANS 2:10, NEW LIVING TRANSLATION)

Have you ever watched an artist paint a beautiful picture? Some artwork is finished in a short amount of time, while other pieces take much longer to complete. The time it takes to finish each piece depends on what is in the picture and what the artist wants to reveal. There are many different kinds of artwork, and each piece is filled with purpose and creativity.

Similarly, our lives are pictures that God beautifully paints to reveal His creativity, love, and beauty. The amazing thing about God is that He never paints the exact same picture. In fact, we are all uniquely made and have details about us that make us special and valuable in His sight. God is the most amazing creator and artist in the world. Everything God creates has purpose and value. He wants to use your life for others to look and say, "Wow, God put a lot of thought into _____ (fill in your name). When I look at _____ (fill in your name), I see God's love and goodness."

God thinks you are beautiful and amazing. He thought about you even before you were born and knew the world would be a better place because of you (see Ephesians 1:4). God has great plans for you (see Jeremiah 29:11). There are ideas, gifts, and talents the Lord has given you that make you unique and unlike anyone else. He has put you in families, friendships, classes, groups, and is taking you places to touch people around you with His love.

Take a moment and think about what you enjoy and are good at. You are good at those things because God created you to be that way. Be mindful of the creative ideas God has placed inside of you and be excited to do the things you are passionate about. You are His masterpiece, and just as God created you, you are filled with His creativity to bring beauty to the world. When the light God has put inside of you shines for others to see, you bring glory to your heavenly Father (see Matthew 5:16). Your life is being painted into a beautiful masterpiece that is filled with detail, excitement, and adventure!

Draw It

Think about yourself as God's masterpiece. Draw a picture of some of the things you see in your masterpiece that make you special and unique.

Additional Scripture References

Psalm 139:13–14   1 Peter 2:9

Isaiah 64:8

Jesus Reveals Himself

"You will seek me and find me when
you seek me with all your heart."
(JEREMIAH 29:13)

G od's Word is true, and He says, "I love those who love
me, and those who seek me find me" (Proverbs 8:17).
Throughout every book of the Bible, God shows Himself to
people in many ways. Do you know what is really amazing?
God still wants to reveal Himself to us today. In fact, He is the
same today as He was hundreds of years ago (see Hebrews 13:8).
Isn't it exciting that if you seek God, He will reveal Himself
to you? God loves you
and wants to spend time with you. Spend time with God by reading the
Bible, praying, worshiping Him, looking for His goodness, and telling
others about Him! God loves it when you do this.

In the book of Acts, after Jesus ascended into Heaven, He revealed
Himself to a man named Saul (who was later referred to as Paul). Saul had
been trying to hurt and imprison Jesus's followers. One day, Saul was on
his way to a place called Damascus when suddenly, a light from Heaven
flashed down. The light was so powerful that Saul fell to the ground and
heard a voice that said, "Saul, Saul, why do you persecute me" (see Acts
9:4)? "Who are you, Lord?" Saul asked. "I am Jesus, whom you are perse-
cuting," he replied. "Now get up and go into the city, and you will be told
what you must do" (Acts 9:5–6).

When Saul got up, he could not see anything and needed others to
help him. As he went into the city, Jesus appeared in a vision to a man
named Ananias. Jesus told Ananias exactly where to find Saul and

instructed Ananias to lay hands on him so that he could see again. When Ananias arrived at the house where Saul was, he laid his hands on him, and sight came back to his eyes. Not only was Saul able to see the world around him again, but when Jesus revealed Himself to Saul, his spiritual eyes were opened as well (see Acts 9:1–19). After encountering Jesus, Saul was forever changed.

Story Time

Sometimes, when I am asleep, I see Jesus in my dreams. I feel peace when Jesus is near. Jesus is holy, nice, and merciful. In one of the dreams, I was in my house, and Jesus appeared. He stretched out His hand to me and said, "I love you." I told Him that I loved Him too. I will always remember His words and great love for me.

Jesus loves you too, and when we invite Him into our hearts, His Spirit comes inside of us. As Christians, we are connected to Him and His Kingdom! Jesus wants to reveal Himself to you more and more. In fact, Jesus loves how children have a lot of faith (see Matthew 18:3–4). Having child-like faith means believing God can do anything (see Ephesians 3:20). At times, people try to boss God around by telling Him what He can and can't do, but this is not child-like faith. God wants us to know that His power and authority are limitless. God loves when we put our faith and trust in Him.

"He called a little child and set him before them, and said, 'I assure you *and* most solemnly say to you, unless you repent [that is, change your inner self—your old way of thinking, live changed lives] and become like children [trusting, humble, and forgiving], you will never enter the kingdom of heaven.'"
(MATTHEW 18:2–3, AMPLIFIED BIBLE)

Write about It

Write a prayer to the Lord. In your prayer, talk to Him about how you want to know Him more. Ask Him to reveal Himself to you more than He has before. You may even want to thank Him for a time you felt Him near.

_____

_____

_____

_____

_____

_____

_____

_____

_____

_____

Additional Scripture References

Psalm 25:14	John 14:21
Matthew 5:8	Acts 2:17–18

God Speaks through Creation

"The heavens declare the glory of God;
the skies proclaim the work of his hands."
(PSALM 19:1)

Lately, I find myself wanting to look up into the sky at the clouds. I love looking for God in nature—especially in the sky. Many times, in scripture, the presence and glory of the Lord came through a cloud. For instance, when Moses led the Israelites out of Egypt, God's presence went in front of them to guide them as a pillar of cloud by day and a pillar of fire at night (see Exodus 13:21). Also, the Bible says that when Jesus returns, He will come in clouds with great power and glory (see Mark 13:26).

Sometimes, when I look into the sky and see the clouds, I feel God's presence. God even speaks through rainbows to remind us of His promises (see Genesis 9:13). Other times, when I admire nature, I feel the Lord speaking to me and opening the eyes of my heart. Isn't it amazing to watch a sunrise or sunset, study the solar system, and observe the weather? God is the most amazing artist and creator of all time!

God also uses His living creatures and nature to teach us more about His power. In fact, the Bible is filled with stories of the Lord using animals to accomplish His will. One time, Jesus and His disciples arrived in a town called Capernaum. Once there, two tax collectors approached Peter and asked him if Jesus paid the temple tax. When Peter returned to Jesus, Jesus began to talk about paying taxes. He told Peter to go to a lake, cast his fishing line, and open the mouth of the first fish he caught. Jesus told Peter that inside the fish's mouth, he would find a coin, and this coin would be enough to pay their taxes (see Matthew 17:24–27). Can you imagine the look on Peter's face when he saw the coin in the fish's mouth just as Jesus said? God is incredible!

"But ask the animals, and they will teach you, or the birds in the sky, and they will tell you; or speak to the earth, and it will teach you, or let the fish in the sea inform you. Which of all these does not know that the hand of the LORD has done this? In his hand is the life of every creature and the breath of all mankind."
(JOB 12:7–10)

Story Time

One day, I was riding in my car and looking out the window at the trees pass by. Suddenly, in the distance, I had a vision of a huge, bright moon. The moon was so big and bright that I could hardly look at it. Quickly, the moon disappeared, and I knew I had seen a vision. As I thought about the vision, I began to understand what the Lord wanted me to know. He was showing me that just as the moon reflects the light of the sun, we are supposed to reflect the light of God's son, Jesus. When we do, we shine brightly for all to see.

"You are the light of the world. A town built on a hill cannot be hidden. Neither do people light a lamp and put it under a bowl. Instead they put it on its stand, and it gives light to everyone in the house. In the same way, let your light shine before others, that they may see your good deeds and glorify your Father in heaven."
(MATTHEW 5:14–16)

Think about It

In your imagination, picture a full moon. Now picture a big dark cloud covering part of the moon. When the dark cloud covers the moon, the light of the moon doesn't shine as bright and it can become difficult to see. The same is true as we shine for Jesus. If we allow dark clouds of pride, anger, jealousy, fear, doubt, and so on to come in, our light can get covered up. When dark clouds try to come toward you, remember that the Holy Spirit living inside of you is more powerful (1 John 4:4). Use the wind from the Holy Spirit to blow away the dark clouds by declaring God's Word and asking for His help.

Faith in Action

Take time this week to look for God in creation. Do you hear the birds singing or feel the wind blowing? Do you see animals playing or notice pictures painted in the sky? God loves it when you look for Him, and He loves speaking through His creation.

Draw It

Draw a picture of one of your favorite places in nature. For example, you could draw the beach, mountains, rivers, fields, woods, deserts, islands, and so on. Think about how you recognize God in the picture you draw.

Additional Scripture References

Exodus 40:35	Psalm 42:1	Isaiah 55:12	Luke 19:40
Psalm 8:1–9	Psalm 69:34	Daniel 6:21–22	Romans 8:19–22
Psalm 19:1–2	Psalm 96:11–12	Daniel 7:13	Revelation 1:7

Angels are Real

"See that you do not despise one of these little ones. For I tell you that in heaven their angels always see the face of my Father who is in heaven."
(Matthew 18:10)

The Lord assigns angels to help and minister to us (see Hebrews 1:14). We should believe God when He says there are angels. The devil probably doesn't want us to believe in God's angels, but Christians should be excited and thankful that God sends help from His Kingdom. Angels bring messages, help believers in need, and work with us to accomplish God's plans. God even has angels in Heaven worshiping with Him right now (see Psalm 148:1-2)!

Also, it is important to know that angels from the Lord don't want to draw attention to themselves. Instead, they honor God and point us to Him and His Word. God talks to us about angels many times in scripture. One of my favorite angel stories is when the angel, Gabriel, appeared to Mary to tell her that she would become pregnant and give birth to Jesus. This encounter was not something Mary imagined; it was real! Gabriel was delivering an important message from God. In return, Mary honored and believed the message from God through Gabriel (see Luke 1:26–38).

Another neat story of God sending angels is found in Acts. While Peter was in prison, the church was praying hard for God to rescue him, and God responded to their prayers in an incredible way. The night before Peter was set to go to trial, an angel came to Peter and told him to get up. As Peter stood up, his chains fell off. He followed the angel out of prison, but at first, Peter thought he was seeing a vision. When Peter realized it wasn't a vision, he went to Mary's house, where people had gathered to pray. Peter knocked on the door, and a servant girl named Rhoda recognized his voice. She told everyone that Peter was knocking at the door, but they didn't believe her (see Acts 12:1–17). "You're out of your mind," they told her. When she kept insisting that it was so, they said, "It must be his angel" (Acts 12:15). Can you believe the church in Acts was so used to seeing angels that when Peter knocked on the door, it was easier for them to believe it was his angel instead of Peter himself?

Story Time

My mom remembers her grandfather telling a story of a time he believed God sent an angel to help him. Years ago, my great-grandfather was driving home very late at night. At that time, there were no cell phones and stores did not stay open late. My great-grandfather was many miles from home when his car ran out of gas. It was extremely dark outside, and there was no one around. As he sat in his car wondering what to do, he saw someone in the distance walking toward him. As the man approached, my great-grandfather could see that he was carrying a gas can. Next, the man walked up to his car and filled it up with gas. My great-grandfather was surprised and extremely thankful. He went to thank the man but saw him walking off and disappear into the night. My great-grandfather always felt that God sent an angel to help him get home that night. Whether or not the kind man was an angel in disguise, only God knows. However, this experience touched my great-grandfather in such a way that his faith in the Lord had forever increased.

"Do not forget to show hospitality to strangers, for by so doing some people have shown hospitality to angels without knowing it."
(Hebrews 13:2)

Draw It

Read the following verse and draw what comes to your mind: "For he will command his angels concerning you to guard you in all your ways" (Psalm 91:11).

Additional Scripture References

Exodus 23:20	Psalm 103:20	Luke 15:10
Psalm 34:7	Matthew 4:6	John 20:11–12
Psalm 78:25	Matthew 24:31	

The Eyes of Your Heart

"I pray that the eyes of your heart may be enlightened in order that you may know the hope to which he has called you, the riches of his glorious inheritance in his holy people, and his incomparably great power for us who believe."
(EPHESIANS 1:18–19)

In the Bible, Jesus healed many people who were blind. When the blind received their sight, they rejoiced and praised the Lord. Just as people can be born blind or become blind, the Bible says that satan blinds the minds of those who do not believe (see 2 Corinthians 4:4). However, when we accept Jesus as the Lord and Savior of our lives, we begin to see with the eyes of our hearts and understand the glory of the gospel of Christ. When the eyes of our hearts can see things that the Lord wants to show us, we begin to praise Him because seeing His glory is amazing.

After Jesus rose from the grave, He stayed with two of His disciples who did not yet recognize it was Him. Sitting at a table with them, Jesus took bread, blessed it, broke it, and gave it to them. Next, the Bible says, their eyes were opened, and they knew Him (see Luke 24:30–31). Jesus had the power to open His disciples' eyes back then, and the same is still true today. When we desire to spend time with Jesus, He opens the eyes of our hearts so that we know Him and better understand His ways.

It is important to always fix our eyes upon Jesus because the god of this world (aka satan) tries to blur our spiritual sight. In fact, satan wants us to see through his lens of darkness instead of God's lens of light. This lens of darkness is filled with doubt, fear, anger, shame, unforgiveness, selfishness, pride, hopelessness, hatred, negativity, and everything not of God. However, there is amazing news! Our God is the Father of lights, and His light pierces through the darkest darkness (see James 1:17 and John 1:5). God's all-powerful lens of light floods our eyes with love, hope, faith, grace, mercy, forgiveness, humility, joy, peace, truth, justice, and everything good. Through God's lens, we see the love He has for us, and see others through the eyes of Jesus.

"So we fix our eyes not on what is seen, but on what is unseen, since what is seen is temporary, but what is unseen is eternal."

(2 CORINTHIANS 4:18)

Story Time

One time, someone started picking on me a lot. This person would call me names, try to take things that belonged to me, and push me around. At first, their actions upset me, but I began praying about what was going on, and one night, God responded to my prayers through a dream.

In the dream, I was on a high bridge that had thousands of snakes covering the ground below. As I stood on the bridge, the person I had been praying for appeared and tried to push me off the side. Holding on to the side of the bridge, I said, "Why are you picking on me?" The person responded and told me it was because they weren't happy with who they were. I suddenly knew that the reason I was getting picked on had nothing to do with who I was, but their own insecurities.

When I woke up from the dream, I felt a new understanding and love for this person in my heart. I felt the Lord wanted me to know the real reason behind this person's actions so I could respond in love. That night, God opened the eyes of my heart so I could see from His point of view and respond with His wisdom. Afterward, I felt free and was able to speak life into this person and pray they would truly see how special God made them.

"In the last days, God says, I will pour out my Spirit on all people. Your sons and daughters will prophesy, your young men will see visions, your old men will dream dreams."

(ACTS 2:17)

Think and Write about It

Has God ever shown you something in the eyes of your heart? It could be something as simple as seeing a rainbow and thinking of God's promises, looking at a situation through faith instead of doubt, receiving a dream, or understanding a Bible verse in a new way. Write about how God has opened the eyes of your heart by revealing Himself to you.

_____

_____

_____

_____

_____

_____

_____

_____

Additional Scripture References

2 Kings 6	John 3:3
Psalm 119:18	Acts 7:55–56
Psalm 146:8	2 Corinthians 5:7

Watching Our Words

"Keep your tongue from evil and your lips from telling lies."
(PSALM 34:13)

As Christians, it is important to be careful to speak words that are filled with love and truth (see Ephesians 4:29). After all, a Christian is someone who is learning to be more Christ-like every day. If we say we are Christians, but speak mean words or talk bad about others, we do not show the love of Christ as we should. When we are mean, people may not want to hang out with us. Also, when our words are unkind, negative, or rude people who are not Christians may not want to get to know the God we say we love. However, when we see others through the eyes of Jesus, we speak words of wisdom, truth, life, and love.

The Bible says, "Don't use dirty or foolish or filthy words. Instead, say how thankful you are" (Ephesians 5:4, Contemporary English Version). It seems like the world is full of bad words in television, movies, music, schools, and sometimes in places that are considered "Christian." When our words do not line up with God's Word, chances are, we do not remember who we are in Christ at that moment.

Sometimes people say bad words because they think doing so is funny or cool, but to God, it isn't funny or cool. Other times, people say bad words because they are acting out of anger or frustration. Nevertheless, it is important to stand up for God and His Word. One way to do this is by not saying or wanting to listen to bad words and asking God to help our words be pleasing to Him.

A good way to know if the words we speak are pleasing to Jesus is by identifying the fruit of the Spirit. Our words should help others feel the love, joy, peace, patience, kindness, good-ness, faithfulness, gentleness, and self-control that comes from the Holy Spirit (see Galatians 5:22–23, New Living Translation). All of us make mistakes and have probably said things we wish we had never said. However, the great part

about mistakes is that we can learn from them. Whenever you mess up, don't think bad of yourself. Instead, ask God to help you be more like Him and do better next time. Try your best to use kind words and be polite. You will be amazed at how much more enjoyable life is by using words filled with life and love!

Story Time

Sometimes I say things I shouldn't say. One time my sister and I were playing a game together. Trying to be funny, I said something that hurt her feelings. I could see that my words really upset her, and I felt sad to see her cry. Immediately, I told her that I was sorry that my words made her upset and asked for forgiveness. What I admire about my sister is that she is very wise with her words and tries not to say things that would hurt other people's feelings. Thinking before blurting out the first words that come to mind takes practice, and I find myself continually asking God to help me watch my words. I am thankful that He is patient with us.

Prayer Time

Father God,

I come to You and ask You to help me speak words that are pleasing in Your sight. Please forgive me when I have said things that have been foolish. Help me to use my words wisely. I ask You to help me forgive others when they say mean words to me or about me. Please help me to pray and love others, even when it is hard. In Jesus' name, Amen.

"May these words of my mouth and this meditation of my heart be pleasing in your sight,
LORD, my Rock and my Redeemer."
(PSALM 19:14)

Faith in Action

Ask the Lord to bring someone that you know to mind. Next, put on your God glasses and think of a way you see the love of God in this person or how the Lord has made them special. Write their name and what comes to mind below. When you see or talk to this person again, encourage them by sharing how you see them through God's lens of love.

_____

_____

_____

_____

_____

_____

_____

_____

_____

Additional Scripture References

Psalm 141:3	Proverbs 16:24	Colossians 4:6
Proverbs 15:1	Matthew 12:36	

The Sword of the Spirit

"Take the helmet of salvation and the sword of the Spirit,
which is the word of God."
(EPHESIANS 6:17)

There are different pieces of armor the Lord gives us for battle against the enemy. The Bible tells us, "Put on the full armor of God, so that you can take your stand against the devil's schemes" (Ephesians 6:11). One of the weapons the Lord gives us is the sword of the Spirit. The sword of the Spirit is not actually a real sword, but God's Word. Did you know that God's Word is all-powerful and sharp like a sword (see Hebrews 4:12)? God's Word brings victory in our lives because it chops up lies of untruth. As Christians, we are instructed to take the sword of the Spirit, and use it to proclaim God's truth to destroy the lies of the devil (see Ephesians 6:17).

Did you know the Bible is alive (see Hebrews 4:12)? This means that each word written inside has life that gives us power from the Lord. I have heard it said that the Bible is the best-selling book of all time. Many people say they believe in Jesus and have a Bible, but never read it. Why not read the best-selling book of all time? Why not read what the author of creation wrote to us? Why not spend time getting to know God? After all, how can we use the sword of the Spirit if we don't spend time being trained in God's Word?

There will always be victory in Jesus, and Jesus is the Word of God. By reading the Bible and asking the Holy Spirit to help us apply it to our lives, our swords get sharper. It is exciting to know that God is training us to be master swordsmen.

Story Time

Sometimes, my school practices fire alarm drills throughout the year. These alarms used to make me feel nervous and scared. I would even tell my parents that I didn't want to go to school because I was worried a fire alarm would catch me by surprise. One day, I decided to ask God to give me peace and remove my fear of fire alarms. A powerful verse to help with worry and fear is, "Peace I leave with you; my peace I give you. I do not give to you as the world gives. Do not let your hearts be troubled and do not be afraid" (John 14:27). Putting this scripture in my sword helps me stand in the peace of Jesus by remembering He is with me. Today, I am no longer scared of fire alarms because of the power from God's Word.

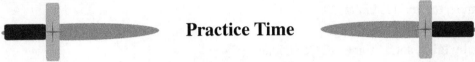 **Practice Time**

It is time to practice using the sword of the Spirit. The sword of the Spirit is all-powerful because the Word of God cannot be defeated. Whenever you feel sad or upset, find a verse about God's joy and speak it out loud. If you feel scared, find a verse that talks about God's power and protection. For example, "Have I not commanded you? Be strong and courageous. Do not be afraid; do not be discouraged, for the Lord your God will be with you wherever you go" (Joshua 1:9). As you speak the verse, imagine the words forming into a powerful sword that pierces through the sadness or fear and chops it into pieces. Every word of God is powerful and can help you or someone you may be praying for feel much better.

Now, pick up the sword of the Spirit and circle one (or more if you want) of the words below that you would like the Lord to help you better understand.

God's Love	**Hope**
Joy	**Faith**
Peace	**Trust**

Next, find the verse that goes along with the word you circled, put it in your sword, and speak it out loud over your life.

~ "For the LORD your God is living among you. He is a mighty savior. He will take delight in you with gladness. With his **love**, he will calm all your fears. He will rejoice over you with joyful songs." (Zephaniah 3:17, New Living Translation)

~ "You make known to me the path of life; you will fill me with **joy** in your presence, with eternal pleasures at your right hand." (Psalm 16:11)

~ "And the **peace** of God, which transcends all understanding, will guard your hearts and your minds in Christ Jesus." (Philippians 4:7)

~ "For I know the plans I have for you," declares the LORD, "plans to prosper you and not to harm you, plans to give you **hope** and a future." (Jeremiah 29:11)

~ "For we live by **faith**, not by sight." (2 Corinthians 5:7)

~ "**Trust** in the LORD with all your heart and lean not on your own understanding; in all your ways submit to him, and he will make your paths straight." (Proverbs 3:5–6)

This week, focus on the scripture you put into your sword. Remember, you chose that word for a reason. Chances are, God will use you to teach others more about Him through the word that was on your heart. God loves you so much.

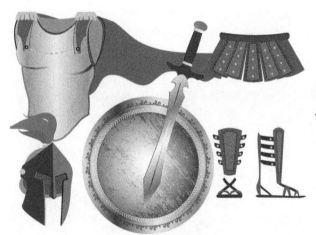

Put on the full Armor Of God, so that you can take your stand against the devil's schemes.

Ephesians 6:11

Additional Scripture References

Isaiah 55:11	Ephesians 6:13
Matthew 4:4	Hebrews 4:12

The Helmet of Salvation

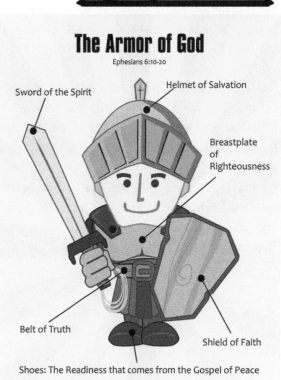

"Take the helmet of salvation and the sword of the Spirit,
which is the word of God."
(EPHESIANS 6:17)

W hen Paul wrote about taking the helmet of salvation, he was talking
to the church. Have you ever wondered why we need to put on the
helmet of salvation if we are already saved? Wearing a helmet physically
protects our heads and spiritually protects our minds.

The helmet of salvation reminds us who we are in Christ
and how we are saved, loved, and forgiven. If we don't know
who we are in Christ or how the blood of Jesus sets us free
from who we used to be, we may not be wearing our helmets
correctly. Remember, the devil doesn't want us to know who
God says we are. After all, he is a liar and tries to trick us into
doubting God's Word. He tricked Adam and Eve in the Garden
of Eden, and he is still up to the same tricks today. This is why
we must be on guard and always take our thoughts or other
people's opinions to the Lord before allowing them to enter
through our helmet of salvation. When we wear the helmet
of salvation, it becomes easier to make our thoughts obey the
Word of God and submit to the Holy Spirit.

Think about It

Imagine that your teacher tells you that you have been chosen
to stand up in front of the school to speak on a certain topic.
At first, you feel special because your teacher selected you, but

65

suddenly you hear questions in your mind asking, "What if I mess up? What if I forget what to say? What if people stare at me?" Next, you start to get nervous and upset. You don't want to feel this way, but the questions won't let up. However, you recognize all of the thoughts bombarding your mind are not bringing peace, and understand the need to secure your helmet of salvation and take out the sword of the Spirit. Wearing the helmet of salvation reminds you of the verse that says, "I can do all this through him who gives me strength" (Philippians 4:13). Your helmet blocks the doubts, fears, and lies that try to come against who God says you are (see 2 Corinthians 10:5), and gives you confidence and peace.

Story Time

One time, my sister and I were running around the house playing with a big blow up hammer. We were having fun bopping each other with it when we accidentally hit a special glass vase that mom got for her birthday. The vase broke into hundreds of pieces, and I saw a look of disappointment on my mom's face. I was really upset with myself, and it made me sad to think I broke something that was special to my mom. I told her how sorry I was, and even though she was not mad at us, thoughts kept running through my head telling me that I was a bad person. I knew my mom had forgiven me, but the thoughts kept telling me that I should not forgive myself. These thoughts made me feel very sad.

Looking back, I know that those thoughts were not from the Lord because the Lord forgives us when we make mistakes and are sorry. The devil is the one who wants us to feel ashamed and guilty. As we put on the helmet of salvation, we know that we don't have to live feeling like we are not good enough or that God doesn't forgive us. Jesus died so that our sins could be forgiven. We are God's children, and there is nothing we can do that would make Him stop loving us.

If you have ever felt worried, ashamed, or like you can't stop thinking about your mistakes, ask God to help you put on the helmet of salvation. A lot of times, we believe there is something wrong with us, but really there isn't. The only thing wrong is that the devil is trying to make us think we're the problem when really, he is the problem. Wearing the helmet of salvation helps us say "no" to the devil's tricks and understand how much Jesus loves us.

Write about It

My helmet of salvation tells me that I am loved by God. Whenever I remember this, I feel

_____

_____

_____

_____

_____

What is something that comes to your mind when you think about who God says you are in Christ?

_____

_____

_____

_____

_____

Additional Scripture References

Romans 8:14   Philippians 4:8

Romans 12:2   Colossians 3:2

2 Corinthians 10:5

The Shield of Faith

"In addition to all this, take up the shield of faith, with which you can extinguish all
the flaming arrows of the evil one."
(EPHESIANS 6:16)

The shield of faith is a little different than most of the other pieces of armor Paul talks about in Ephesians. Instead of putting on the shield of faith, we are told to take up the shield of faith. Raising up the shield of faith requires effort on our part. When we have faith, we don't just think or talk about God and His Word; instead, our lives begin to look like what we believe in (see James 2:17).

Faith is confidence the Holy Spirit gives us to trust and hope in God's promises. Choosing to trust God even when we don't know what will happen, puts our faith into action (see Hebrews 11:1). Raising the shield of faith protects us from the enemy's attacks because it is made up of everything God can do.

An example of faith in action is seen when looking at the life of Abraham. The Bible says, "By faith Abraham, when called to go to a place he would later receive as his inheritance, obeyed and went, even though he did not know where he was going" (Hebrews 11:8). Abraham was called by God to leave his country and travel to a distant land so that he could receive the promises God had in store. When Abraham understood what the Lord was telling him to do and obeyed, his faith was put on display for all to see. Even when Abraham did not see the full picture, he knew God did and trusted in His protection and power.

Just as Abraham was called out of the land where he was born to a land of promise and blessing, we are called to do the same. This world is not our home, and we are told to leave behind the ways of the world and follow God's ways. Throughout this beautiful journey of trust, faith, and obedience, God leads us into His promised land. At times, it may not be comfortable, and it may not be what we want to do, but God is pleased by our faith that shows we trust He knows best.

"And without faith it is impossible to please God, because anyone who comes to him must believe that he exists and that he rewards those who earnestly seek him."
(HEBREWS 11:6)

Story Time

God really loves us, and He wants us to have fun, but sometimes we have to leave things behind to follow God, even if it means moving to the other side of the country. Yes, a few years back, I had to move from my home all the way to the other side of the country.

At first, it was hard to think about moving. I loved my home, church, town, friends, and school. I didn't want to move away and asked my parents why we had to leave all of these things behind. My parents told me that God was telling us to move, and we needed to trust Him even when it didn't make sense (just like Abraham did). They also said, many times, God doesn't give us the entire picture of what is to come, but as we put our faith in His leading, He guides us each step of the way.

At first, moving to a different place was hard, but over time, I saw that God really did have great plans for our family. Since moving, I have made new friends and memories. I also live in a beautiful town, go to a wonderful school, and have grown a lot in my relationship with God. My family moved to honor God, but God moved my family because He knew what was best for us. As we trust God's lead and step out in faith, God grows us in ways we would never have experienced if we had merely stayed comfortable following our own plans. By raising our shield of faith, we partner with God and begin to see Him work in exciting ways. Be eager to step out in faith and go on adventures with God. You will be amazed at what unfolds and how He uses you.

"The LORD directs our steps, so why try to understand everything along the way?"
(PROVERBS 20:24, NEW LIVING TRANSLATION)

Draw It

Draw a giant shield of faith! After you draw it, fill it in with words about God's strength, power, character, and promises.

Additional Scripture References

Mark 11:23	1 Corinthians 16:13	James 1:3
Luke 17:5	2 Corinthians 5:7	James 1:6
1 Corinthians 2:5	Colossians 3:2	

Citizens of Heaven

"But we are citizens of heaven, where the Lord Jesus Christ lives. And we are eagerly waiting for him to return as our Savior."
(PHILIPPIANS 3:20, NEW LIVING TRANSLATION)

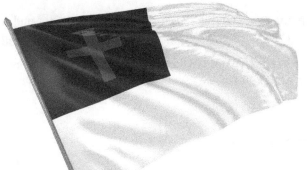

God created Heaven, and Jesus describes it as "paradise" (see Luke 23:43). Jesus tells us that He is preparing a place for us there and that He is the only way into Heaven (see John 14:2 and 14:6). Heaven is a place filled with God's love, glory, and holiness. In Heaven beauty, worship, peace, life, and joy fill the atmosphere. Also, God's throne is in Heaven, where Jesus is seated at His Father's right hand (see Isaiah 6:1–3 and Colossians 3:1).

When we become Christians, we become citizens of Heaven. A citizen is someone who is a member of a certain place. Citizens are asked to obey the laws of their country. They also get to enjoy the rights, protection, and benefits their country offers.

One day, we will live in Heaven forever, but until then, we are used to help others understand a little more about where we are from. For instance, have you ever met someone from another country or region and noticed they do things differently than you? They may eat different foods, speak a different language, have unique traditions, hold certain beliefs, and so on.

As Christians, we are also from another place and do things differently than those who are not from our homeland. This is why it's important to understand our heavenly culture. Our culture looks different than the culture of the world. Heaven's culture is filled with God's love and truth. When we seek after God's heart, Heaven's culture

71

becomes more and more natural to us. As we bring Heaven's culture to Earth, light invades the darkness of a world that needs Jesus to set them free.

Story Time

Not too long ago, there was a movie I wanted to go see at the theater. The movie didn't have a bad rating, and it looked good in the previews. However, when the movie started, I quickly realized it was very inappropriate, and my spirit was bothered by it. Next, I decided to do what any citizen of Heaven would do; I left the theater. At first, I felt guilty for going to the movie but quickly realized that Jesus was proud of me for standing up for what I believed best honored Him.

Question and Answer Time

1. As citizens of Heaven, and God as our leader, it is important that we try our best to obey God's commandments. What do you think are some of the rules we should follow as citizens of Heaven?

_____

_____

_____

2. As citizens of Heaven, the Lord protects us. Can you think of a time when you felt God protecting you?

_____

_____

_____

3. As citizens of Heaven, we get to experience the benefits/blessings of God. What is a benefit that comes with being a citizen of Heaven?

_____

_____

_____

_____

_____

Additional Scripture References

Psalm 33:13	Acts 1:11	Philippians 11:27	Revelation 15:3
Matthew 3:2	Romans 12:2	Colossians 3:2	
Matthew 24:14	Ephesians 5:15–17	Hebrews 11:16	

Light and Darkness Do Not Mix

"For you were once darkness, but now you are light in the Lord. Live as children of light (for the fruit of the light consists in all goodness, righteousness and truth) and find out what pleases the Lord. Have nothing to do with the fruitless deeds of darkness, but rather expose them."
(EPHESIANS 5:8–11)

At the beginning of time, when God created the Heavens and the Earth, the Earth was empty and dark. God saw the darkness and said, "Let there be light," and He separated the light from the darkness (see Genesis 1:1–4). God's light is filled with life, goodness, power, and love. Did you know that God is even called the Father of the heavenly lights in scripture (see James 1:17)?

The Bible says that before we are saved, we are in darkness, but when we accept Christ, we become members of His Kingdom of light (see Ephesians 5:8). Also, God's Word is described as a lamp to our feet and a light to our path, and Jesus calls Himself the light of the world (see Psalm 119:105 and John 8:12). As followers of Jesus, the light of the world shines brightly inside of us to guide and protect us from things hidden in the dark. When we ask the Holy Spirit to help us obey God's Word, His light shines through us so that we can see where to go, what to do, and know the difference between God's truth and the lies of darkness.

Think about It

For a moment, imagine you are in a room that is completely dark. You need to see the way out, but because of the total darkness, you do not know which way to go or what is around you. Next, picture a flashlight appearing in your hands. When the flashlight turns on, the darkness filling the room is broken by the light shining forth. Suddenly, you can see your surroundings and which way to go. It is pretty amazing how just a little bit of light can pierce through a huge room of darkness.

Now, imagine Jesus's power shining brightly inside of you like a radiant flashlight. When you walk in the light as He is in the light, it is easy to see what is hiding in the dark and the steps Jesus wants you to take. Jesus's light is all-powerful, and when His light shines in the dark, the darkness will never be stronger than it (see John 1:5).

Remember, Jesus's light inside of you is greater than the darkness in the world (see 1 John 4:4). Make sure to turn on your flashlight by asking the Lord to help you walk in His light. As you shine brightly for Jesus, there is hope for those in the darkness to have their eyes opened to the truth of God's goodness, mercy, grace, and love (see Matthew 5:16).

Story Time

Once, some kids were playing pretend on the playground, but what they were pretending to play was not good. I thought to myself, "Could I see Jesus playing this?" In my spirit, I knew what they were doing represented the kingdom of darkness, and I did not want to pretend along with them. Even though the other kids thought the game was no big deal, in my spirit, I knew that God's light would not mix with the darkness in the game. Instead of joining them, I decided to walk away. It felt good to obey the pull of the Holy Spirit inside of me and represent the Kingdom of Light. After all, light and darkness do not mix.

Draw Lines to Connect the Words that Go Together from the Left to the Right

Praying for someone who is sick	Light
Lying to your parents	Light
Being a bully	Light
Sitting beside someone who is eating alone	Dark
Obeying your parents	Dark

Additional Scripture References

Ecclesiastes 2:13   Psalm 27:1   1 Peter 2:9

Walls Don't Make a Church—People Do

"Don't you know that you yourselves are God's temple and that God's Spirit dwells in your midst?"
(1 CORINTHIANS 3:16)

Putting on a cape doesn't magically make you Superman, and sitting in a church doesn't magically make you a Christian. Carrying a Bible, wearing a Christian t-shirt, necklace, or even decorating an entire house with the word "Jesus" doesn't make you saved. There is so much more to being a Christian than going to a church building each week or dressing up in Jesus clothes. Being a Christian isn't about looking the part on the outside, it is about asking Jesus to help us shine for Him from the inside out.

Of course, we should go to church and be thankful to have a building to worship in with other believers. Going to church is amazing, and God loves His Church! Yes, it's good to carry a Bible, wear Christian attire, and decorate our homes with reminders of Jesus, but these things don't have the power to save us. Jesus is the only one who has the power to save. When we believe in Him, we begin to trust and obey Him. Only Jesus can change us from the inside out.

When Jesus was alive, the Scribes and Pharisees were groups of Jews that spent their time studying Jewish teachings. However, even though they studied God's Word, they didn't allow it to change them on the inside. Instead, many were filled with pride. They dressed in special clothing, prayed long prayers, told people what to do, and were given the best seats to sit in—all to get attention (see Matthew 23:1–12). Even though they told people to obey God's Word, they did not truly love God or others (see Matthew 23:28). Nevertheless, Jesus seeing their hearts, told the crowds and His disciples that the Scribes and Pharisees did not do the things they preached about (see Matthew 23:1–3).

Jesus wants us to know that being a Christian isn't about looking better than others; it's about loving God and loving others. After all, as one Body of Christ, we are all on the same team. Let's treat each other as teammates and work together to bring glory to God instead of trying to glorify ourselves. Celebrating who we are in Christ doesn't just happen on Sundays as we gather in a building. Because Jesus lives in us, we get to be with Him each and every day!

Story Time

One day, I decided to eat an entire bag of cotton candy. As I ate each fluffy piece of dyed sugar, it tasted so good, but afterward, I got a terrible headache. I knew that my head was hurting because of all the sugar I had eaten, and my body was trying to let me know.

Taking care of our bodies is important, but we also must take care of our spiritual bodies. The Bible says that we are temples of God, and He lives in us (see 1 Corinthians 3:16). At times, we may do things that seem fun or popular, but these things actually go against what Jesus would do. This is when we make choices that are not healthy for us. If we keep doing things that go against who we are in Christ, chances are, we won't feel as spiritually healthy (just like when we eat too much cotton candy). However, when we rely on the Lord to guide and nourish us, we grow strong in Him. Realizing that we carry God's Spirit inside of us brings a refreshing reminder of how important it is to take care of ourselves and make wise choices. We are a walking, talking house of God. Let's honor the Lord by doing our best to keep our spiritual home clean and healthy.

Poetry Time

Create an acrostic poem. An acrostic poem is created when the first letters of each line spell out a word that describes the subject.

Example

Great

Outstanding

Dad

Now it's your turn. Write an acrostic poem that describes a healthy house of God. (**Hint**: examples of letter "u" words include: unselfish, uplifting, united, understanding, unwavering, unbreakable, and upbeat.)

C

H

U

R

C

H

Additional Scripture References

Matthew 22:37–39	2 Corinthians 13:5
Acts 17:24	Ephesians 3:17
1 Corinthians 6:19	Philippians 2:12

Helping Those in Need

"And do not forget to do good and to share with others,
for with such sacrifices God is pleased."
(Hebrews 13:16)

The Lord cares about our every need. In fact, we can talk to Him about anything because He cares about the smallest details of our lives. When Jesus lived on the Earth, He cared for those who were hurting, lost, poor, sick, and sad. It didn't matter if they were the most popular or least popular. Jesus didn't care about being popular with people; instead, He loved everyone and wanted to please His Father in Heaven.

In Matthew 25, Jesus spoke about helping those in need. He said that when we see someone who is hungry, thirsty, without a place to stay, in need of clothes, sick, or even in prison, we should help them by sharing God's love. When we help those in need, it is like we are doing those things for Jesus as well (see Matthew 25:31–40).

God is love, and His love is such a powerful force. Jesus said that when we love one another the way He has loved us, everyone will know that we are His disciples (see John 13:34–35). God's love comes in many different ways. At times, showing God's love is simply being there to listen to a friend who is going through a hard time, sharing God's wisdom and truth to someone who is lost, being a friend to someone playing alone on the playground, or giving a hug to someone who is sad. Other times, showing God's love means giving money or food to the poor, going on mission trips, donating clothes to those in need, praying for someone who is sick, or telling others about Jesus.

Lastly, we should help others because we want to and not because we feel like we have to. The more we love the Lord, the easier it becomes to show God's love to the lost and hurting world around us. After all, loving God and loving people encourages us to put the needs of others before our own, just like Jesus did.

"Do nothing out of selfish ambition or vain conceit. Rather, in humility value others above yourselves, not looking to your own interests but each of you to the interests of the others."
(PHILIPPIANS 2:3–4)

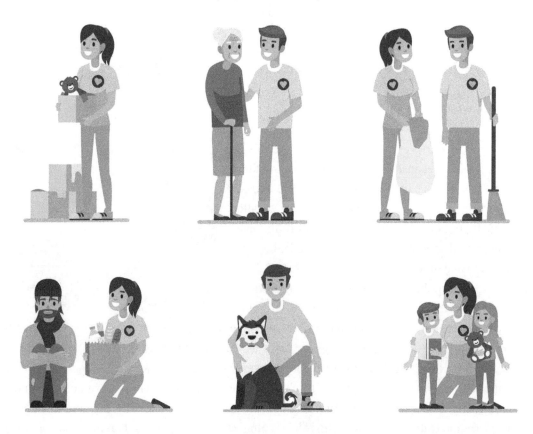

Story Time

One time, I was playing with a group of friends. We decided to divide up into teams to play a game. I was chosen to be a captain of one of the teams. As a captain, I got to pick who I wanted on my team. Normally, the best players are chosen first because everyone wants their team to win. However, the players selected last sometimes feel sad because everyone else gets chosen before them. I knew how it felt to be chosen last and decided to do something different this time. Instead of picking the best person to be on my team first, I decided to pick the one who was usually chosen last. It was wonderful to see how happy it made the person feel to be selected first. It also made me feel good to see them feel valued, and I knew that was more important than winning any game.

Prayer in Action

Do you know someone who is in need or going through a hard time? Write their name and what they need prayer for below.

_____

_____

_____

_____

Next, take a moment and pray to God on their behalf. If no one comes to mind, pray for God to touch anyone who needs His comfort and help.

Father God,

I come before You and thank You for _____ (insert their name). I ask for You to comfort and provide for _____. I thank You that Your Word says, "And my God will meet all your needs according to the riches of his glory in Christ Jesus" (Philippians 4:19). Thank You for meeting the needs of _____ and revealing Your great love to them. In Jesus' name, Amen.

Additional Scripture References

Proverbs 19:17	Hebrews 6:10
Romans 12:13	Hebrews 13:16

God Our Healer

"LORD my God, I called to you for help, and you healed me."
(PSALM 30:2)

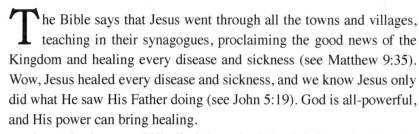

The Bible says that Jesus went through all the towns and villages, teaching in their synagogues, proclaiming the good news of the Kingdom and healing every disease and sickness (see Matthew 9:35). Wow, Jesus healed every disease and sickness, and we know Jesus only did what He saw His Father doing (see John 5:19). God is all-powerful, and His power can bring healing.

Jesus also instructed His disciples to heal the sick through the power of the Holy Spirit (Matthew 10:8, Luke 10:9). As Christians and disciples of Jesus, the power of God can flow through us in the same way because God's power is still at work today (see Romans 8:11). One of the gifts the Holy Spirit gives is healing, and we are told to lay hands on the sick and pray for them to recover (see 1 Corinthians 12:9 and Mark 16:18). God uses different ways to bring about healing such as through prayer, doctors, medicine, eating healthy, rest, and so on. Healing can happen instantly, over time, or when we get to Heaven.

"The thief comes only to steal and kill and destroy; I have come that they may have life, and have it to the full."
(JOHN 10:10)

God wants not only to heal our physical bodies, but also to bring healing to our hearts (who we are inside) so we can look more like Him. Sometimes bad choices can make us sick in body and in spirit. Other times, we get sick because we live in a world that is imperfect. However, when we are sick or hurt, knowing that God is increasing our character, faith, and trust in Him helps us get through each day (see Romans 5:3–4).

In chapter three of Acts, an incredible story of healing is recorded. One day, Peter and John were going to the temple to pray. On the way, they saw a man who had been crippled since birth being carried to the temple gate to beg for money. However, Peter and John didn't have any money to give the him. Instead, Peter told the man to stand up and walk in the name of Jesus Christ of Nazareth (see Acts 3:6). Instantly, the man was healed and began walking around praising God. When others saw how the man had been miraculously healed, they were amazed. Peter said to them, "By faith in the name of Jesus, this man whom you see and know was made strong. It is Jesus' name  and the faith that comes through him that has completely healed him, as you can all see" (Acts 3:16). God's love is amazing, and there is power in the name of Jesus (see Acts 3:1–16).

Story Time 1

One time, when I was six years old, my family was shopping at a store. Looking around, I noticed an older lady sitting on a bench with a dog. I asked my parents why the lady had a dog in the store, and they told me that she was blind and had a service dog to help her get around. As I looked at the lady, I felt God's love for her. I started to remember stories in the Bible of how Jesus healed those who were blind, and I wanted to pray for Jesus to heal her as well.

With my parents' permission, I walked up to the blind lady and kindly asked if I could pray for her. At first, she looked surprised, but then welcomed the offer for prayer. Next, I prayed and asked God to heal her and restore her sight in Jesus' name. Although the lady was still unable to see after the prayer, she was very thankful, and her service dog was too! He began jumping on me and licking me all over. I have heard that service dogs don't normally act this way, but I think he could sense the love of Jesus in my heart and was saying, "Thank you."

I sometimes wonder how this lady is doing today. Even though I didn't see her healed, I am thankful that I prayed and did what God's Word tells us to do. Regardless of whether or not someone gets healed, I can pray boldly because praying in faith is not about me or my strength, but about God's strength and my willingness to obey His Word.

Story Time 2

Another time, I prayed for healing was when I was waiting for a music lesson to begin and noticed my teacher came in holding his wrist. He looked like he was in a lot of pain, and I saw that his hand and wrist were very swollen. A bone looked like it was nearly sticking out of his skin. My teacher said that he had fallen and hurt his wrist several days before. A lady standing nearby told him that she thought it was broken and that he should go to the doctor to get it x-rayed. I wanted to pray for my teacher when I saw how much pain he was in.

After the lesson, my mom and I asked if we could pray for his wrist, and my teacher agreed. We laid our hands on his injury and began to pray for God to heal him in Jesus' name. After the prayer, my teacher was very appreciative, and it looked like he had tears in his eyes. Days later, when we came back for the next lesson, my teacher said that he needed to talk to us. Excitedly, he began moving his hand and wrist around perfectly. To our amazement, there was no more swelling or evidence of it ever being injured! My teacher said, "Thank you so much for the blessing you spoke over me. After you left, my wrist began to heal, and the pain left." He was overwhelmed with the love of God that touched him that day. Thank you, Lord, for Your healing power!

Faith in Action

This week, ask the Lord to show you someone you can pray for who is hurt or sick. You can go up to them and pray with them for healing, or you can pray for them on your own when you are alone with God. Insert the name of the person that comes to mind below and pray the following prayer:

Father God,

I believe in Your healing power. I come to You today and ask You to heal _____.
Please give _____ comfort and strength. I ask for You to help _____ be healthy in body and strong in spirit. In Jesus' name, Amen.

Additional Scripture References

2 Chronicles 7:14	Mark 5:34
Isaiah 53:4–5	3 John 1:2
Jeremiah 30:17	

Joy in Trials

"Consider it pure joy, my brothers and sisters,
whenever you face trials of many kinds,
because you know that the testing of your
faith produces perseverance. Let perseverance
finish its work so that you may be mature and
complete, not lacking anything."
(JAMES 1:2–4)

Even though we may go through difficult times in life, the Bible tells us to count these times as joy. Going through hard times is not always easy, and it can be hard to find joy when things don't go right. Sometimes, what is happening doesn't seem fair or make sense. The devil tries to use trials to stop us from being who God called us to be. However, God is greater and can use the hard times for our good as we grow spiritually and rely on His strength and wisdom to help us through. Even in hard times, we can learn to love more and understand just how much we need God each and every day.

In the book of Daniel, the story of Shadrach, Meshach, and Abednego talks about a time of great trial and faith in God. Shadrach, Meshach, and Abednego were Jews who loved the Lord. In fact, they loved God so much that they would not bow down and worship King Nebuchadnezzar's golden idol even though the penalty was being thrown into a blazing hot furnace. When King Nebuchadnezzar found out that the men would not bow down to the idol, he was furious and ordered Shadrach, Meshach, and Abednego to be thrown into the blazing hot furnace.

As they were taken to the furnace, the flames were so hot that the soldiers near them died. Nevertheless, Shadrach, Meshach, and Abednego put their faith and trust in the Lord as they stood in the flames. Finally, when the king looked into the furnace, to his surprise, he saw four people walking around unharmed by the fire. Immediately, King Nebuchadnezzar knew that Shadrach, Meshach, and Abednego's God had come to protect them. After they came out of the furnace, King Nebuchadnezzar declared that the God of Israel would be honored, and he promoted Shadrach, Meshach, and Abednego (see Daniel chapter 3).

Today, God still has the same power as He did when Shadrach, Meshach, and Abednego were alive. When we go through difficult times, it is important to ask God what He wants to teach us and how we can come out looking more like Jesus. After all, as we walk through fire with Jesus by our side, we come out burning with the light of Christ more brightly than ever before.

"And we know that in all things God works for the good of those who love him,
who have been called according to his purpose."
(ROMANS 8:28)

Story Time

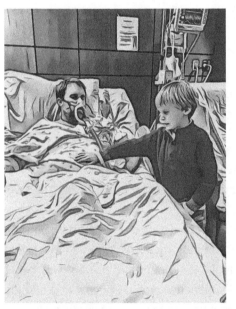

A few years ago, my dad got really sick. I went to visit him in the hospital, and he looked hurt, weak, and tired. It made me sad to see my dad sick and in the hospital. He described his pain as a fire inside of him that could not be put out. The only thing I could do was ask God to heal him.

For weeks, I prayed over and over again for God to heal my dad, and many other people prayed too. The song we continually worshiped to while my dad was sick had lyrics that spoke about walking through fire with our hands lifted high as God strengthens us. During this time, God also gave my great-aunt a vision of Jesus carrying my dad through fire, and my dad even saw a vision of Jesus as the Lion of Judah walking through fire. It was obvious the Lord was revealing He was with my dad and carrying him through this time of trial and fire. In the Bible, Shadrach, Meshach, and Abednego were in a literal fire, and God was with them, and the same God—our wonderful God—was confirming that He was with my dad as well.

As weeks went by, Christmas was approaching and my dad was still in the hospital. One afternoon right before Christmas break, I got home from school, and my mom told me there was a Christmas gift waiting inside. As I walked through the kitchen, I saw my dad sitting on the couch! Having my dad home was the most wonderful Christmas present ever!

Although my dad's sickness was difficult for my family, I learned to pray harder and depend on God's strength more than ever. God taught me that even in the hard times, He comforts us and hears our prayers. Looking back, I see how much joy I felt when my dad came home and realize how thankful I am for my family.

Write or Talk about It

Write or talk about a difficult time you or someone you know has been through. For example, maybe you were nervous to start a new school year, were sick or hurt, got made fun of, and so on. Write or talk about what helped you get through it and what God taught you.

_____

_____

_____

_____

_____

_____

_____

_____

_____

Additional Scripture References

Joshua 1:9	Psalm 46:1	1 Peter 5:7
Psalm 32:7–8	Isaiah 12:2	
Psalm 34:17	Romans 5:3–4	

God's Wisdom

"If any of you lacks wisdom, you should ask God, who gives
generously to all without finding fault,
and it will be given to you."
(JAMES 1:5)

God's wisdom comes when we want to know God's ways and hear His instruction. Growing in wisdom takes time. When someone enters a new grade in school, they don't instantly know everything they need to know just by sitting in a seat. Instead, as the year goes on, the student gradually learns from their teacher's instruction. For Christians, God sends the Holy Spirit to be our teacher (see John 14:26). Over time, as we understand and obey His teachings, we graduate to higher grade levels of maturity in Christ.

Growing in Christ is not always about how many years we have been alive; it is about learning and obeying God's instruction. Someone may say they have been a Christian for twenty years but not obey their teacher, the Holy Spirit. Jesus was not old when He began His public ministry, but He had always obeyed His Father. Even when Jesus was a child, the Bible says He was filled with wisdom and God gave Him favor (see Luke 2:40 and Luke 2:52). Regardless of whether you are old or young, you can be filled with and grow in God's wisdom. Can you imagine how much wisdom you will have by the time you get to be grandparent if you ask the Holy Spirit to lead you each day of your life (see Romans 8:14)?

"Don't let anyone look down on you because you are young, but set an example for the believers in speech, in
conduct, in love, in faith and in purity."
(1 TIMOTHY 4:12)

In 2 Chronicles, God appeared to King Solomon and said, "Ask for whatever you want me to give you" (see 2 Chronicles 1:7). In response, Solomon asked God for wisdom and knowledge so that he could be a good leader for God's people (see 2 Chronicles 1:10). It pleased God that Solomon did not ask for wealth, treasure, or for God to hurt his enemies. Instead, Solomon wanted to be able to understand what God needed him to understand. In return, God not only gave Solomon wisdom and understanding, but He gave him more wealth, treasure, and honor than any other king before had ever received (see 2 Chronicles chapter 1). Like King Solomon, when we ask God for wisdom and put Him first, He not only gives us wisdom but His blessings and favor fill our lives as well.

Story Time

One Sunday, my family and I were visiting a church. My sister and I went to the children's church, but I noticed what the teachers were teaching was different than what the Bible said. I felt in my heart that this was wrong and went against God's Word. After church, I spoke to my family about what happened. We all agreed that what they were teaching was not right according to the Bible. Together, we prayed for the teachers and children. We thanked the Lord for His wisdom so that we could know God's ways. What I learned is that when we draw near to God, He teaches us and gives us understanding. Even church leaders can make mistakes at times. This is why it is important to take everything to the Lord and ask Him for wisdom to know His truth, instead of believing everything we hear right away.

Write and Encourage

Think about someone you know that shows God's wisdom. Write their name here:

_____

_____

_____

_____

How can you see God's wisdom in their life?

_____

_____

_____

_____

_____

God loves it when we encourage others. Write a short note or draw a picture and give it to the person you thought of. In the note or picture, share how you see God's wisdom in their life.

Additional Scripture References

Proverbs 3:7	Proverbs 9:10	James 3:17
Proverbs 3:13	Matthew 6:19–21	1 John 2:27
Proverbs 4:6–7	2 Timothy 2:15	

Forgiving Others

"Bear with each other and forgive one another if any of you has a grievance against someone. Forgive as the Lord forgave you."

(COLOSSIANS 3:13)

Sometimes, other people do things that hurt our feelings. In fact, the Bible says that we have all sinned and fallen short of the glory of God (see Romans 3:23). However, Jesus who never sinned loved us so much that He died for us so we could be made right with God (see 2 Corinthians 5:21).

We all make mistakes and mess up, but God still loves us and is by our side to help us learn and grow. When others hurt our feelings or do things that aren't nice, it is important for us to forgive them as well. We are called to treat others the way God treats us, and God treats us as loved and forgiven. At times, people may do or say mean things that Jesus would never do or say; however, if their words and actions don't line up with God's Word and heart, those things aren't the truth. We must remember who we are in Christ and pray for those who try to upset us (see Luke 6:28).

God wants to tell us who we are and how much He loves us. When we know how amazing we are in God's eyes, the hurtful words and actions of others don't sting as much. The more we know how much we have been forgiven and who we are in Christ, the easier it is to forgive others and hurt for them instead of being hurt by them.

Forgiveness doesn't mean we ignore what has happened, and forgiving someone doesn't mean what they have done is right. When we sin, it's not right, but we know that God will forgive us and help us do better if we ask.

Forgiving someone means that regardless of what they have done, we will not allow their actions to have power over us or take away the love of God in and through us.

Think about It

Holding onto unforgiveness is like having a deep cut that never heals. We may try to put a bandage on it or ignore it in hopes that it will disappear, but when we feel the pain, we quickly remember the wound is still there. Over time, the cut could even get infected or start to spread to other areas. If we had simply gone to the doctor, the cut could have been healed by Jesus, our great physician. Only Jesus can truly heal our hurts. As we think about the deep wounds Jesus experienced on the cross so that we could be forgiven and free, and ask God to help us forgive others as He forgave us, we allow God's power to heal our hearts and set us free from the wounds of unforgiveness.

Story Time

My dog has always been one of my best friends. He was a part of our family the day I was born and has been with me my entire life. I love spending time with him. However, my dog is getting older now, and sometimes he doesn't act like himself. One day, I was sitting outside with him (near his food), when all of a sudden, he jumped and bit me on the face. I was shocked, and it hurt really bad. My face had bite marks on it, and blood ran down my cheek. My parents immediately took me to the doctor. Thankfully, the bite wasn't deep enough to need stitches, but the doctor gave me medicine to prevent the wound from getting infected.

At first, I was upset with my dog and hurt by what he did. I felt like I couldn't trust him anymore and like I had lost my best friend. As days went by, I began to realize that it wasn't that my dog didn't love me, but because he was getting older, his mind wasn't thinking the same way it used to. With the Holy Spirit's help, I was able to forgive my dog for biting me. Of course, I am much more careful now around him, but deep down I love him, and it feels good to be able to forgive him.

Write about It

Have you ever been in a situation where your feelings were hurt? Write about what happened and how you felt once you forgave the other person.

_____

_____

_____

_____

_____

_____

_____

_____

_____

_____

_____

Additional Scripture References

Psalm 86:5   Matthew 6:14–15   Mark 11:25   Ephesians 4:32   Colossians 3:13

Stepping Out of Our Comfort Zones

"I can do all this through him
who gives me strength."
(PHILIPPIANS 4:13)

THE RIGHTEOUS
ARE BOLD
AS A LION

·PROVERBS 28:1·

In life, sometimes we find ourselves having to do things that push us out of our comfort zones. During these times, we must look to God and allow His strength to help us through. Being a Christian doesn't mean that we always have to act like everything is fine. In fact, as Christians, we shouldn't think this way at all. God loves us so much and wants us to come to Him to talk about what we are going through. The more we realize how little we are and how *big* God is, the more we depend on His power to help us through whatever comes our way.

In the Bible, Queen Esther was someone who was called out of her comfort zone and used by God in a powerful way. Did you know that Queen Esther was not always royalty? In fact, Esther was born Jewish, and when she was young, she became an orphan when her parents died. Thankfully, her cousin, Mordecai, took her in and raised her.

One day, King Xerxes began searching the land for a queen, and out of everyone, He chose Esther. It must have been a big change for Esther to leave her old life behind and become royalty. When Esther became queen, she did not tell King Xerxes about her Jewish heritage, and one day, a man named Haman, who was an enemy of the Jews, came up with a plan to kill the Jewish people. However, Esther's cousin, Mordecai, overheard the evil plan and sent a message to her. He asked Esther to go before the king and beg for mercy so that the Jewish people could be saved.

The problem was that people were only allowed to approach the king if he called for them first. Esther knew if she went to the king without being called, she could be put to death.

Nevertheless, Esther wanted to stand up for the Lord and the Jewish people, even if that meant risking her life. Queen Esther put her faith and trust in God, and the king agreed to protect the Jewish people. As a result of Esther's bold faith and trust in the Lord, the Jewish people were saved (see Esther, chapters 1–8).

Like Esther, when we honor God's Word and are obedient to do what He tells us to do, He gives us wisdom, favor, strength, and courage. At times, stepping out of our comfort zone may feel uncomfortable, but God is there to help us every step of the way. After all, He sees the end from the beginning and knows the beauty that is in store for those who put their trust in Him.

Story Time

One day, I was watching an online video about a certain game. All of a sudden, the person talking in the video said a bad word. I immediately turned the video off, but I felt ashamed to have heard the bad word. I wanted to tell my mom what happened but was worried she would be upset with me. In my spirit, I felt grief and wanted to be honest about what I had heard. It was uncomfortable telling my mom what happened. I didn't want her to be disappointed in me, but I knew God would want me to do what was right.

I finally got up the courage to tell my mom about what happened, and to my surprise, instead of being upset with me, she was proud of me. My mom told me that she saw how upset I was and how my heart was filled with truth and honesty. I felt relieved and loved after talking about what happened. This situation helped me understand that when we love God, doing what is right is more important than secretly trying to get away with things that go against His Word, regardless of the consequences. Obeying God shows that we want to walk in the truth, and His truth will always set us free (see John 8:32).

95

Write about It

Write about a time you stepped out of your comfort zone. Maybe it was when you started a new school year, played in a game, moved to a new home, spoke in front of others, told the truth when it was hard to, or shared about your faith in Christ.

_____

_____

_____

_____

_____

_____

_____

_____

Additional Scripture References

Deuteronomy 31:6	Isaiah 1:17	Galatians 6:9
Psalm 34:14	Isaiah 26:3	
Proverbs 3:5–6	Isaiah 41:10	

God's Sparkling Jewels

"As you come to him, the living Stone—rejected by humans but chosen by God
and precious to him—you also, like living stones, are being built into a spiritual house to be a holy priesthood, offering spiritual sacrifices acceptable to
God through Jesus Christ."
(1 PETER 2:4–5)

Have you ever gone digging or hunting for gemstones? Most gemstones are formed within the Earth's different layers. When gemstones are first dug up, they don't look as shiny because they have been buried in darkness and covered by dirt for a long time. After a gemstone is discovered, there is a process it goes through to bring out the beauty that is hiding inside. Did you know that part of a gemstone's value is based on the way it radiates light? However, before it can reflect light, the stone must be cleaned, cut, and polished. The more the stone is cleaned, cut, and polished, the more beauty it displays as it reflects light.

In a similar way, we too are God's precious gemstones. At first, we were born into a world filled with sin and darkness (see Psalm 51:5). This sin and darkness covered us just like dirt covers gemstones before they are found. Nevertheless, God is the master miner! He knows exactly when each of us is ready to be discovered and uncovered.

After being stuck in the dirt and darkness of the world, once we give our lives to Jesus, He lifts us out of the dirt and holds us firmly in His hands. Next, Jesus gets to work making us beautiful and sparkly in His sight. First, He cleanses us by washing away and forgiving our sins (see Hebrews 10:10). Next, He begins to cut out the places that do not look like Him. As the Lord chisels away areas that block our beauty, we become more humble and dependent on His strength. Although the cutting phase may feel uncomfortable, God is teaching us to get rid of the places that have covered up our value, worth, and

identity in Him. Finally, the Lord polishes us by teaching us who we are and showing how He has put His fingerprint on our lives. Even though we may find ourselves continually asking God to cleanse, cut, and polish us, we know that deep inside, He sees our treasure, worth, and value.

Like gemstones, the Lord has brought you up out of the darkness and into His marvelous light to radiate His glory (see 1 Peter 2:9). Each day along this journey called life, as you grow in Him, you sparkle more and more for the world to see. Remember, His light is shining in you, and He created you to reflect His light for all to see. Wherever you go, know that you are His treasured gemstone that brightens the world with His heart of love and beauty.

"The Lord their God will save his people on that day as a shepherd saves his flock.
They will sparkle in his land like jewels in a crown."
(ZECHARIAH 9:16)

Story Time

A few years back, my family went mining for gemstones. We found many neat fossils and stones as we dug through the dirt. At first, we didn't know what type of stones we'd discovered because they had not yet been cleaned, cut, or polished.

After digging and collecting the stones, we took them to a gem cutter. The gem cutter examined the stones and told us we found amethysts, rubies, garnets, and many others. Next, the gem cutter cleaned, cut, and polished some of the stones, but this process took time to complete. When we went back to pick up the gemstones, they looked completely different from the dirty stones we dug up! In fact, they were beautiful and sparkled like treasure.

Years later, my sister decided to open the bag of stones from our trip to reexamine what we found. When she dumped out the bag, she noticed a grayish looking rock in the shape of a golf ball. On the outside, it was dull and looked like a rock you would see by a creek. However, we noticed that it seemed to be hollow, and decided to break it open to find out what was inside.

Excitedly, we gave the rock to my dad, and he broke it in half with a hammer. To our surprise, the inside was filled with sparkling white crystals! It turned out, this was not an ordinary rock, but a geode! The hard outer shell hid the sparkling beauty that was within. Even though we had kept this beautiful geode for years, we had no idea what was inside.

This story reminds me of who we are in Christ. At times, it may take a little while to recognize exactly who He has created us to be, but the Lord looks deep within and sees the beauty we possess. It is amazing how just one touch of God's power can burst open even the hardest of hearts and free us from the dirt that has covered up our true value for so long.

"You will be a crown of splendor in the Lord's hand, a royal diadem in the hand of your God."
(ISAIAH 62:3)

Draw It

Draw a picture of a beautiful crown with gemstones on it. You are God's crown of splendor!

Additional Scripture References

Isaiah 61:10   Matthew 21:42   Ephesians 5:8–9

Final Thoughts

Congratulations on finishing the book! I hope that it encouraged you and brought you closer to God. Rejoice and be glad because God loves you and has made you special. God gave you a life, a meaning, and a purpose. Be bold for Christ and keep walking in His freedom. May the Holy Spirit guide and protect you. Praise God, Hallelujah! God loves you, and I hope you love God!

God bless you,
Carter

Reflections

Listed below are several questions followed by my own personal answers. After you read each question and answer, think about how you would answer the same question. You can even write your response in the space provided below each one. As time goes by, continue to reflect on the questions and answers that come to your mind.

1. What are the first words that come to mind when you think about God?
My answer: "Holy and Glorious"

Your answer: _____

_____

2. What do you feel God has called you to do?
My answer: "I feel like God has called me to save lives for His Kingdom and stand up for what is right."

Your answer: _____

_____

3. What is one of your favorite Bible verses?
My answer: "How beautiful on the mountains are the feet of those who bring good news, who proclaim peace, who bring good tidings, who proclaim salvation, who say to Zion, "Your God reigns" (Isaiah 52:7)!

Your answer: _____

_____

4. What do you think Christians need to know more about?

My answer: "A lot of Christians don't know what God has called them to do, what God is doing in the spiritual world, or the difference between right and wrong. It seems we need to ask God to help us know more about all of these things."

Your answer: _____

_____

5. What book in the Bible or Bible story is one of your favorites to read?

My answer: "2 Kings (though all of the books of the Bible are amazing)."

Your answer: _____

_____

6. What was your favorite part of this book?

My answer: "My favorite part of the book is the section that talks about Jesus being our friend. Jesus inspired me to make this book because He wants others to know how much He loves us and wants to have a relationship with us."

Your answer: _____

_____

7. What does being set free in Christ mean to you?

My answer: "When Christ sets us free, we no longer allow the devil or sin to hold us down, but depend on God's strength to help us through each day. It also means walking according to the Spirit and not the flesh."

Your answer: _____

_____

Credits

CPSIA information can be obtained
at www.ICGtesting.com
Printed in the USA
LVHW060321180119
604308LV00003B/12/P

9 781545 656433